# BEFORE YOU
# WAKE

Center Point
Large Print

**This Large Print Book carries the
Seal of Approval of N.A.V.H.**

# BEFORE YOU WAKE

*Life Lessons from
a Father to His Children*

## ERICK ERICKSON

Center Point Large Print
Thorndike, Maine

This Center Point Large Print edition
is published in the year 2017 by arrangement with
Hachette Books, a division of Hachette Book Group, Inc.

All quotes from the Bible refer to
the English Standard Version.

The text of this Large Print edition is unabridged.
In other aspects, this book may vary
from the original edition.
Printed in the United States of America
on permanent paper.
Set in 16-point Times New Roman type.

ISBN: 978-1-68324-606-0

Library of Congress Cataloging-in-Publication Data

The Library of Congress has cataloged this record
under LCCN: 2017041315

Some believe it is only great power that can hold evil in check. But that is not what I have found. I have found that it is the small things, everyday deeds of ordinary folk that keep the darkness at bay. Simple acts of kindness and love.

—Gandalf the Grey, *The Hobbit*

Hear, O Israel: The Lord our God, the Lord is one. You shall love the Lord your God with all your heart and with all your soul and with all your might. And these words that I command you today shall be on your heart. You shall teach them diligently to your children, and shall talk of them when you sit in your house, and when you walk by the way, and when you lie down, and when you rise. You shall bind them as a sign on your hand, and they shall be as frontlets between your eyes. You shall write them on the doorposts of your house and on your gates.

—Deuteronomy 6:4–9 (ESV)

# CONTENTS

# INTRODUCTION

To my children, Evelyn and Gunnar,

Sometimes we encounter suffering. We don't know why it happens. When it does, some people will come to you and say, "God is testing you." To others, "God is setting you up for something if you weather the storm." But sometimes hard times are just hard times. There are no lessons to be learned. And sometimes, only in retrospect do you see those lessons.

In time, your memory of challenging periods of your lives will start to fade. You will remember bits and pieces, but maybe not the whole. You'll no doubt remember bits and pieces of this past year of our lives. This past year was the hardest year for our family. It has weighed on your parents so much.

In April 2016, I spent a week in the hospital trying not to die. My lungs had filled up with blood clots. My blood oxygen level had fallen below 90 percent. I could not breathe lying down or standing up. Walking left me gasping for air. For months I thought it was allergies, but it got worse and worse, until finally your mother forced me to go to the doctor. The doctor sent me to the hospital for a CT scan and I never left. Within hours I was being treated like a stroke victim, administered tissue plasminogen activator, then lots of blood thinners. I looked like the victim of a car wreck, with a single bruise stretching from my shoulder to my hand.

Gunnar, perhaps by the time you read this you will have forgotten, but for the last year you have been increasingly worried about me. You are upset I work too much, insistent that I play with you to get me out of the office, and mad at my boss, "Mr. Pete," for working me so hard.

As it turned out, I wasn't the only one you and your sister began to worry about. While I was in the hospital, your mother traveled to Arizona to the Mayo Clinic for a checkup on her lungs. The doctors found spots growing and in June, performed a lung biopsy. While I have clots in my lungs, your mom has a rather uncommon form of lung cancer. Thankfully, an oral chemotherapy she is taking is shrinking the growths.

In the midst of these twin medical crises, the 2016 presidential campaign was in full swing and I was a conservative who did not support Donald Trump. Protestors showed up at our home. People sent us hate mail. They called my office daily demanding I be fired. Everybody was convinced I had destroyed my career. Our house had to be protected by guards. You two were yelled at in the store by a man angry with me for not supporting Donald Trump. At school, other kids made sure you knew your dad was not liked in their household. Some of them wondered aloud if something bad would happen to us.

For a time we stopped going to church because we couldn't make it from Sunday school to the sanctuary without someone stopping us to give us a piece of their mind about politics. One day toward the end of 2016, I went up to bed late, looked at your mother, and said, "I don't know if I'm going to survive this year." Your mom had a near meltdown. "I've made a deal with God," she said. "He can't take both of us." Here we were, both of us just over forty, and for a time it seemed we both had a death sentence.

I would lie awake at night wondering what I needed to do to make sure you two would be okay if something happened. I realized that if I died tonight and you googled me, you would come away with an awful picture of me, much of it untrue. But some of it is and these are things with which I must reckon. But nothing you'd find on the internet would give you a real picture of who your father is, why I have raised you as I have, and how much I want for you to be a better person than me.

I realized I needed to write down the things I want you to know about me; the things I want you to know about life; the reasons we believe what we believe and have raised you accordingly; and I really just want you to know me. Being told you might die has a way of shaking you to your core and making you reprioritize things in your life.

Above all else in this universe, know that your mom and I love you. If something should ever happen to us that means we are separated from you by the chasm of eternity, we want to see you again and be with you. But in the meantime we want to make sure you are raised lovingly and properly. I want you to know how we come into your room at night and just watch you sleep. I want you to know in the quiet hours of darkness we sometimes cry because we know your body, heart, or soul is hurting. I want you to know that our love for you is so deep and wide that you will never truly be able to fathom it till you have children of your own.

This most painful year we have endured together has made us stronger as a family, more tender to friends, and has both provided valuable lessons and made me aware I need to share those and other lessons with you. I needed to write this book for you. I have written two books in the past. One I did not really want to write. The other felt necessary, if not personal. But none were like this. This is a book I need you to read—perhaps not at this moment, but to open later, like a time capsule. That is why I am compelled to write this book. If I should die before you wake, I want you to know these things are real and true.

Love you always,
Dad

# BEFORE YOU
# WAKE

# • ONE •
# WAITING FOR BATMAN
## *God Has a Plan and It May Not Be Yours*

I was sitting in the mud crying. The rain was falling gently. I remember it was quiet. In my lap was Evelyn, our one-year-old. How could I explain to her that her mother, Christy, was dying? Doctors had just told me she had six months to live.

When you get married you don't think about being widowed. You read stories in *People* magazine about other people's tragic lives—celebrities who die young or random families who encounter unspeakable heartbreak. Here I was, covered in mud, snot, rain, and tears, with a baby girl in my lap patting me as if to tell me it was okay. It was happening to me. I had become a country music song.

Christy and I got married in October 2000. Angie, her mother, had died when Christy was a kid, but Christy was old enough to remember her. Her mom made tape recordings for Christy and her younger sister and wrote personal notes for them to open later. Christy's mother, grandmother, and others in her family all had breast cancer. We knew the odds were against Christy. To change fate, Christy decided to undergo a prophylactic mastectomy soon after our wedding. She didn't have cancer, but given the odds, we knew she would get it.

On January 19, 2001, Christy had her surgery. The next day I watched the presidential inauguration from the hospital as my wife recovered. The muscle damage was so bad the doctors could not complete a reconstruction. So we had more surgeries to go. Over the next several years, Christy would have several more reconstructive surgeries, as the first few never really took. Then we had Evelyn, and Christy needed another one.

But by the beginning of 2006 we were in a good place. I had practiced law for six years, five of them in a law firm. While I was at my law firm, some friends started a political website, RedState, in 2004 and it quickly found an audience. I started to write for it. That November, MSNBC was looking for a conservative blogger to fly up to New York to blog the last week of the election. They reached out to RedState and I was the only one who could go. After informing my bosses, a partner in my law firm came in my office, closed the door, and asked the question that changed my life. "Do you know the definition of a dumbass?" he asked.

I laughed. "No," I replied.

He stared right at me. "You," he said. "You hate practicing law. You need to go find a job in politics. It's what you love."

That conversation changed my life. In November 2005, I left my law firm and soon began working full-time as RedState's editor. By 2006, Christy's surgeries were done, my life had stabilized in a job I loved, and we had our first child. But the light at the end of the tunnel turned out to be the headlamp of a fast-approaching train.

"You've got to come get me. I feel like I'm dying," Christy told me over the phone. That was the Friday before Labor Day in 2006. She served as the assistant to the president of my alma mater, Mercer University, and was curled up in a ball on the floor of her office's bathroom. I rushed to the campus. When I found her, she was pale, cold, clammy, and sweating. I carried her across campus to her boss's doctor in the medical school. He said her symptoms were consistent with either a pulmonary embolism or a gallbladder attack. We went to the emergency room for a scan of her lungs.

The doctors found no pulmonary embolism so it had to be a gallbladder attack. They did, however, note some curious spots in her lungs, but those could be dealt with later. Sure in the knowledge it was just a gallbladder attack, we drove off the next morning to Gulf Shores, Alabama, to spend the week with my in-laws. Christy was in agony the entire time. Evelyn, perhaps sensing her mother's distress, never fussed during the five-hour drive.

The next day I took Christy to a nearby emergency room. Turns out she had a buildup of gallstones in her bile duct. When I suggested we drive back home so she could have surgery, the local doctor matter-of-factly told us she'd be dead by the time we got there. Instead they whisked her off to emergency surgery.

That Labor Day, Christy recovered from surgery at the beach, and I got to play with Evelyn and build memories I would not otherwise have had. Evelyn had been born in August 2005 as I was winding down my law practice. Between leaving my law firm and starting at RedState full-time, I took a job in Washington, D.C. As I commuted to Washington every week, I had few memories of Evelyn's first year. One week I'd be home for three days. The next week I'd be home for four. One of the only memories I have of that time is Evelyn's first smile. She was in her crib, sick, but looked up at me and smiled. I got a picture of her second smile and that memory has never left me. Christy finally told me I was either going to kill myself or she was going to kill me. I quit that job and started full-time at RedState on July 1, 2006.

Now, several months later, here I was at the

beach and all I had to do was play with Evelyn. We spent a lot of time in the pool. I read through Harry Potter and made my way through Dr. Seuss multiple times. We hung out at a hole-in-the-wall barbecue joint. I had a beer, she had a bottle, and we shared french fries. "Dad!" she could gurgle. I have no idea what else she was saying, but that one I knew.

We made it home after a week at the beach, relieved that Christy's health scare was behind us. On our home answering machine we found a message from the first emergency room, in Georgia. They found something "upon further review" of Christy's scan. It was the blocked bile duct. All we could do was laugh.

The days turned cooler. The leaves fell off the cherry tree in the backyard. Thanksgiving came and went. Just before Christmas, Christy's doctor suggested she have a follow-up scan because of those spots in her lungs. I remember her coming home that day. I had just turned the corner in the hallway. I knew something was wrong the moment I saw her; she had the look on her face she gets when she does not want to tell me bad news.

"I have to pack a bag and go to the hospital," she said. When scanning her lungs, doctors found a blood clot in her jugular vein, which is not exactly a common place for a blood clot to be lodged. They were going to put her in a hospital room and pump her full of blood thinners. The combination of the spots in her lungs and this blood clot had made the doctors suspicious. They wanted to make sure she did not have cancer. Given her family history, it was plausible.

Just before Christmas in 2006, Christy had a lung biopsy. It was a miserable surgery.

To make matters worse, on the day Christy headed into the operating room, my partners at RedState announced we had to close up shop. After the Republicans lost control of Congress in November 2006, our ad revenue plummeted. As Christy was about to wrap up surgery, I was coming to the realization I was about to be unemployed for the first time since law school.

Then the doctors came out. They summoned my father-in-law, mother-in-law, and me down a corridor that housed a series of small, windowless rooms. In the room they placed us in, there were a couple of chairs, a table, and a phone, and I am pretty sure there was a Bible. It was like a scene from a movie.

The surgeon told us that the pathology report did not look good. It appeared that not only did Christy have cancer, but it was an aggressive one that had spread to her lungs. Having looked it over several times, they were convinced that was the case, and they were further convinced that she probably had no more than six months to live.

It had started to rain outside. The roads were

slick and a terrible accident happened. The doctor had to excuse himself to go help in the emergency room. My in-laws did their best to keep it together. I went to be with Christy as she woke up from surgery.

As she came to, I told her what the doctors said. I did not cry, but my voice quivered. She was having none of it, which made me more determined to force the gravity of the situation into her head. I walked with her as they wheeled her to a private room. Our preacher and his wife met us at the door. Christy's parents were crying. Then it dawned on me I had to go get Evelyn from daycare.

I rushed out of the hospital into the rain, got in my car, avoiding eye contact with anyone at daycare, and ferried Evelyn to our house. But I was done. I could not handle it anymore. I was out of a job and six months from being a widower. I pulled Evelyn out of her car seat and sank in the mud. On my knees all I could do was cry. I held that baby tight and she patted me on the face as if to tell me it was okay. But it was not okay.

How was I going to explain this to her? In six months, when suddenly I would be the only one around, how was she going to know what happened to her mom? I finally got up the strength to get her in the house. I carried her upstairs, put her in dry clothes, and laid her in her crib. I went to my office and tried to start sending emails with the prognosis. My dad and oldest sister were coming to take over. When they got there, I could go back to the hospital. Until then, the house was cold and dark and quiet, except for me crying. Being alone with dark thoughts is never good, but I had no choice.

I finally made it back to the hospital a few hours later. Christy was in her room and she was still too hardheaded to believe she was dying. She would not even entertain the thought of it. She was far more concerned about what I was going to do. I was sure it had to be the pain medicine talking.

"You know what you need to do?" she asked. "No," I moaned. "You need to be a catapult," she replied. "You have been finding people and ideas and throwing them out there for other people to talk about. You need to find a job to do that. You should be the guy who throws other people and good ideas into the arena." I liked the sound of it. I had no idea how to do it.

We kept talking and talking. Christy might not have thought she was going to die, but we talked about the things you do not talk about unless confronted by death. What sort of person should Evelyn have as another mother; what sort of job I needed; should we change churches; how Christy wanted Evelyn to remember her; the things we needed to do in the next six months—we talked about it all.

Around 10:30 p.m. the surgeon returned. He was on his way home and wanted to check in. "We had the pathologists go back over the biopsied material," he said. "We don't think it is cancer, but we do not know what it is. We have decided to send it off to the Mayo Clinic for examination."

Was this a sick joke? Another wave of emotion hit me. I was happy, crying, nauseous, excited all at once. It was like the end of a roller coaster. Hallelujah! The doctor left and all we could do was sit there in silence, letting the day soak over us. The feeling of nausea was the last to leave. All I could do was keep kissing Christy. Then, of course, we had to go back through all the things we had just talked about and make sure the decisions we had made still held up. They did.

I did not even think about looming unemployment that night. I left the hospital so Christy could sleep. My snoring would have kept her up—her and the rest of the floor. The next morning I had an email waiting for me from one of my partners at RedState. He was delighted by the doctors walking back reports of Christy's death and also had news of his own: We had gotten an offer to sell RedState. The site would not have to close after all. Over the week of Christmas, we negotiated the sale of the business and I agreed to stay on as the editor for three years.

Christmas of 2006 was one of the happiest in

my life. Some say it was luck. Some say it was the natural flow of things. I say it was providential. I had never been one of those people to write out plans. When I was a lawyer, most people in my firm got swept up in the craze of writing one-, three-, and five-year plans of where they wanted to be. I never had wanted to do that. I go where the good Lord leads. I have never put myself on a career path. I work hard and opportunities have been placed in front of me.

Case in point: In 2007, I got elected to our local city council. No one actually ran against me. My single-minded issue was shutting down massage parlors in town that served as fronts for human trafficking.

That year, we decided it was time to try again at growing our family. By now we knew Christy had a genetic clotting disorder, so she would have to go on blood thinners during her pregnancy. Thankfully she could give herself the injections. Gunnar was born on December 9, 2008.

Gunnar's birthday will live in infamy in the family. We knew Christy would have to be induced. Given her health, the doctor wanted to be in control of everything. Christy's mom came down to stay with Evelyn and we went in to the hospital around six o'clock in the morning. I had my iPad, the hospital had Wi-Fi, and *The Dark Knight* was out on iTunes. I set my iPad to download the movie, sat back, and fell asleep.

I do not remember much of the next few hours, other than my wife yelling at me to stop snoring. Allegedly, nurses were popping their heads in to see what the awful noise was. Yes, my wife was having contractions, had not yet had an epidural, and I was on the couch sound asleep, sawing logs, waiting for Batman. Kid? Pfffft. Batman was coming out.

Gunnar came that afternoon—before Batman, I might add. Hospital Wi-Fi sucks.

Now we had our family. With all the other health concerns, we knew Gunnar had to be our second and our last. Health issues and babies behind us, we could grow the family. As we got into 2009, Christy became more convinced it was time for her to stay home with the kids.

As much as she loved her boss and her job, after several years of hair-raising adventures in health care, she was done. That raised all sorts of problems. We were on Christy's health insurance and the cost of buying our own plan would have been tremendous. I had not had a pay raise since RedState had changed owners; we were already living paycheck to paycheck. All we could do is pray.

I know scripture says, "be still and know that I am God," but it can be really hard to be still. Waiting on God can draw out your worst impatience. But sometimes God works fast.

Within seventy-two hours of Christy deciding

29

to leave her job, I got an email from a lady named Michelle at CNN. She wanted me to call her. She would be producing a new show for John King and wanted to know if I would like a job. She said she had been involved back in 2004 with finding the bloggers for MSNBC. She had eventually made her way to CNN, but had followed my career. They were looking for an outside-the-Beltway conservative and hoped I would fit the bill. A day after that, my boss at RedState's parent company called to tell me I was getting a raise. It equaled the income Christy was giving up. God is good.

CNN flew me to New York to meet with the executives at the network. We negotiated a reasonable deal for three years. Next thing I knew, I was on TV. Not only that, but I was surrounded by people I had grown up watching. Paul Begala, James Carville, Mary Matalin, Donna Brazile, Wolf Blitzer, David Gergen—you name it.

They were, truth be told, rather skeptical of a "firebrand conservative blogger." I, of course, had grown up thinking most of them were the enemy. Over three years, though, I learned it is possible to have good friends with whom you disagree politically.

At CNN I learned a lot. My boss, Lucy, had one rule of thumb: Believe whatever you want to believe, but be respectful. I did not always live up to that, but I tried. I also realized some of these "enemies" were the nicest people ever. We may have disagreed on politics, but I could hang out with them and we all had something in common. We also shared a common cynicism about people on TV who had never done anything but claimed to be experts.

I had, in my law firm, run political campaigns, developed polling, designed mail and commercials, developed grassroots plans, etc. Suddenly I was on television with people who had run presidential campaigns and people who had done jack but were somehow "political strategists." The camaraderie between those of us who had actually done real jobs in politics transcended partisanship. This was my tribe.

A year before I joined CNN, the local news-talk radio station had called to see if I could fill in for one of their hosts. He had been arrested in a drug raid. That day of fill-in turned into three months of getting up at 5 a.m. to do radio from six to nine in the morning. It lasted three months, at which point they hired a guy who had worked up in Atlanta. I got paid in expired gift certificates to local restaurants.

A year later, the radio station asked me to come back. The local host had been promoted to the Dallas market. I filled in again for a few months and the president of the Cox Media Group happened to listen. He had Greg, the company's radio consultant, call me to see if I might want a weekend radio show. "Absolutely not," I told Greg. I already had enough to do and did not want to give up my weekends.

Greg called back later to see if I might at least like to fill in for Herman Cain. That was a no-brainer. In October 2010, I drove up to Atlanta and filled in for Herman Cain's evening radio show. When the show was over several people walked in the studio. I knew immediately the visions of a long radio career were burning up like an asteroid entering the atmosphere.

Instead, the program director informed me that they did not really want me to have a weekend radio show. Cain was running for president and they wanted to see if I would like his job. I did not hesitate. "Absolutely," I said. Then added, "But I need to ask my wife first."

On January 11, 2011, I started my very own radio show. I was the first person at WSB to get a five-day-a-week show who had not started out on the weekend, so they told me. It turned out that during the Great Depression, my aunt Lela had also worked at WSB. She would sing and play the piano on Saturdays and Sundays for people going to synagogue and church.

Life thereafter was on cruise control. I did my show from 9 p.m. to midnight, five nights a week. The first week was during an ice storm. I slept on the floor of the station, had no phone callers, and talked for three hours every night. Eventually, I started filling in for Rush Limbaugh. I moved my TV gig over to Fox News. I never saw 2016 coming.

The best-laid plans are often not the ones that take shape. God has a plan and it may not be yours. You can be waiting for Batman one minute and the next find yourself in the hospital trying not to die.

But there is also something else. Had I to do it all over again, I would. I would do it in a heartbeat. I would marry the same woman and we would have the same kids and we would make the same mistakes, if not more, and learn the same and more lessons. We would love and live and try not to die.

A lot of people spend their lives second-guessing decisions. I just go where the good Lord leads. The burdens, the heartache, the tragedy, the suffering, and the joy are all parts of life. There is no use second-guessing things already done because they are not within your power to control. There is no use having a pity party over cancer or blood clots or a lot of other terrible things, because those things are not in your control. If there is one lesson I have learned above all others, it is that things not within your control are things not worth getting worked up about. They just are.

When you head out into the world, you are going to be confronted with a lot of choices. Many of them will be overwhelming choices. Many of them will be choices where you realize you know no one who can relate to those choices from whom you can seek advice. All you can do is pray about it and proceed. You may make the wrong choice. There are choices I have made that I have realized were wrong. But it was no longer within my power to undo them so there was no point in lingering on them.

Life just comes at you. President Calvin Coolidge used to say that when ten problems were bounding down the road at you, if you just stand still nine of them will bounce off the road before they get to you. I think he was right. And I think you have to chart the road on which you wish to travel, then let life or the Lord, depending on your perspective, lead. Sometimes you will find yourself in the whirlwind. Sometimes you will find yourself snoring in a hospital room waiting for Batman.

# TWO

# SUMMER IN THE SOUTH

## *To Suffer Is to Live*

Here is what is happening as I am writing this. Exactly seven days ago, Gunnar was in surgery having his tonsils and adenoids removed. Five days ago, Christy had surgery to reattach her retina. For the last week, I have gotten up at midnight, 4 a.m., and 6 a.m. to give Gunnar pain medicine. For the first few days, Christy had to have pain medicine, too.

Thankfully, my in-laws stayed with us for the week. I cooked and stayed up through the night. They did the laundry, got Evelyn back and forth to school, and helped her with her homework while taking care of Gunnar and Christy during the day. I worked all day. In addition to being up all night, I still had my radio show to do in the evening.

I found myself staying up till midnight to give Gunnar his first dose of medicine and, in the quiet part of the night, doing as much work as I could—including writing this. Every time I wake Gunnar up to give him his medicine, he screams and fights me for close to twenty minutes. He will spit out his medicine multiple times. We will go through multiple shirts. Then he will finally wear down, be still, and submit.

I am not sure there is a better analogy to God. "Be still and know that I am Dad," to paraphrase the scripture. What my kids do not see is me staying up after Gunnar has gone back to sleep and wiping tears out of my eyes. It hurts me to see my wife and my kids in pain. Gunnar's screams are so terrible. He cannot talk. He holds his throat with his hands and tries to cover his ears with his elbows. When that does not work, he moves his hands back and forth from covering his ears to covering his throat. I knew the doctor said his ears would hurt after having his adenoids out, but I had no idea how badly.

One of the things I see happening more and more in the world is people trying to sterilize themselves from pain. They want to shield themselves. I want to shield my kids from pain. I want to shield my wife from pain. But pain is a part of the process. How do we really appreciate joy if we have not known misery? How do we appreciate comfort if we have not known pain?

If nothing else, there is certainly a theology to pain. I have a preacher friend who tells a story about pain from an old church. There were three women, all of whom had cancer. The first took an oral chemotherapy. Her hair stayed. She had no nausea. But she had chronic pain, a rash, and sores in her mouth. The second woman took traditional chemotherapy. She lost weight, had nausea, and her hair fell out. The third woman had done it all and nothing worked. All she had to do now was prepare to die.

The first woman looked at the second and, despite her sores and pain, was glad she kept her hair and figure. The second looked at the first and thought losing her hair was a far better trade than being in pain and aching all the time. They both looked at the third woman and realized that though they were going through a rough patch, at least their treatment was working. The third woman looked at the first two and was glad to be done, relieved her struggle had ended, and was prepared for her maker.

All three women looked at a fourth woman in the church who had lost her son in a bombing. They all thought that, though they had terrible struggles, at least they did not have to deal with the pain of losing a son. That fourth woman consoled herself that her son would never have to go through the struggles of those other women or see his own mother struggle.

I cannot tell you how often I have dwelled on this. I see in my own life and my family's life a change in our perspective on others' suffering through our own. There is a couple not far from us who have a gravely ill son. His older brother had the same illness and died. They are the nicest, Godliest people. Evelyn prays for them regularly and her mood is often affected by whether or not that family has had a good day or bad. She often openly wonders why God would do that to a family. We can look on our struggles and think that at least our children, despite pain and discomfort, are with us.

We also see how much more empathetic and sympathetic we are. It is not a boast, but a reality. We know now from our own struggles that sometimes a home-cooked meal for another family in need is the best thing to do. In our suffering, even though it is different, we are able to relate to other people's suffering. Their pain and struggle shape our prayers.

I remember a preacher coming into our Sunday school class once to talk about suffering and death. He told us of a lady in his church who had been in a car wreck. Her daughter died. He said people flooded the lady's hospital room to comfort her as she lay there broken, bruised, and crying. No one could console her. Then the door opened and her best friend walked in. She climbed into the hospital bed and held the lady, and they cried.

These are abstract things when you have not experienced them. And many of us have not. In our quest to shield ourselves from suffering and pain we are losing an ability to relate to and care for other people. To suffer is to live. Living requires suffering. The steady flow of conformity, comfort, and convenience takes away appreciation for the good times. It takes away the good times.

In sixteen years of marriage, Christy and I have only had a few where we were not dealing with her health or mine. The first six years of our marriage were punctuated by one hospital stay or another. We had Evelyn and then Christy's near-death experience with her lung biopsy. Then we had Gunnar.

Through Christy's pregnancy with Gunnar, she had to take blood thinner shots every day. There are only so many jokes you can make about the bruises before you go gallows humor. It looked like I was beating her up. For nine months she took those shots and then Gunnar came into the world. The last traumatic act of his birth was his grandmother declaring he looked far more like the delivery room doctor than me. That was awkward.

After Gunnar's birth, it was smooth sailing for several years. But last year the bottom fell out. It began, as so much pain and misery begins, with CrossFit. In 2015, I decided to get back in shape. I hate the gym. I do not mind exercise. But the gym can be so boring. CrossFit looked fun. I discovered I had several prominent members of the CrossFit community who read my website and listened to my radio show. They were very encouraging. So I did it.

I actually enjoyed it, but God help me, I could not keep up. I gasped for air like a fish flailing about on the floor of a boat. I kept telling myself it would get better. It did not get better. By Christmas I was done. I could not keep up. I was going to a trainer a few days a week so I bought him a set of CrossFit weights and medicine balls and decided we could take it slow, but keep at it. It never got better. I took Gunnar to see *Star Wars: The Force Awakens* and it literally left me breathless—so breathless my wife rushed me to the emergency room thinking I was having a heart attack. I thought I was just having some sort of cosmic near-sexual experience now that Star Wars was finally back. According to the doctor, everything was fine.

It had to be allergies. Of course, it was not. It was the clots. Christy had the cancer and I had the blood clots. I remember getting checked into the cardiac ICU and the doctor on the floor happened to look at my scan. "Have you taken this body to the morgue yet?" he asked. When they told him it was me, he popped his head in to congratulate me on being alive. A year after my clotting episode, I had another lung episode and had to go to the emergency room. The doctor on call came into the little holding room where I was and asked how I was still living, considering my scans from last year. It is never a good feeling when everyone tells you that you should be dead.

Remember the three women in my friend's church? It occurred to me that the greatest ministry we have for other people is often our suffering. In our family's struggles, others have found a purpose. We have had friends who made it their mission to pray for us. Others cooked for us. Others picked up the kids from school when we could not drive.

Our suffering helped other people find a use, often at moments they otherwise felt useless. Our suffering also let others know they really did not have it as bad as they thought. For that matter, even in our suffering Christy and I realized how much better we still have it than some.

By being open about our struggles and our health, others felt comfortable finally opening up about their struggles. Christy and I found ourselves becoming more compassionate to others than we had ever been before. We were never self-absorbed, but we certainly did not appreciate the strains and struggles in people's lives like we now do.

Had we not suffered, I also would have never learned to make chicken and dumplings. It is Christy's favorite comfort food. One of the ladies in our Sunday school class brought us a pot of it after our hospital surgeries. Christy started craving it, but was too shy to beg for it. I finally had to take it upon myself to learn how to make it. I even learned how to roll out the dumplings all by myself. If we had not gone through what we went through, I would still not know how to do that.

Something else that became even more distinct after our struggles was a recognition that we can find common ground with people we might otherwise not be able to relate to. Living in the spotlight, I have made it a habit to be open about my life. I try to relate to my listeners on my radio show. They are an extended family. But in writing about our struggles, I found that others who might disagree with me on politics were reaching out with prayers and well wishes.

All of this makes me worry about the future. Human beings have become so good at sterilizing themselves and desensitizing themselves to suffering. When people suffer, they want it to end. If the suffering will not end, they are ready to end their lives.

I hear more and more stories of people who, after discovering they have a terminal disease, do not want to suffer. They do not want their families and friends to have to deal with the suffering. They do not want anyone to have their last memories be of their loved one suffering. So they end things before the suffering gets under way.

I understand that desire. Christy, having at a young age seen her mother die of cancer, has been very insistent that if she gets to that point, she wants someone to end it for her so we do not have to witness her suffering. I am in no position to judge or throw stones. I do wonder, though, if we are depriving others of some purpose or peace we do not understand by not going through the suffering.

By depriving people of our suffering, are we also depriving others of the chance to find their purpose, or to realize their lives are better than they think? Are we, by ending it before the agony, depriving a child of the impetus to go to medical school to find cures to suffering? As I see how much my family's suffering has helped others in our community, the more I wonder what will happen as society eliminates suffering altogether.

The struggle for life and survival is inspirational in ways submission and retreat are not. Truly, to each his own. I know from my and my family's suffering that there are others who have suffered far more, and while I may be more empathetic, I still cannot truly relate to their level of suffering. But I also see how people's suffering opens doors and eyes and hearts.

In my freshman year of college I had to sit around a table with a professor and other freshmen to talk about suffering, pain, joy, and evil. At the age of eighteen, it finally dawned on me that I probably would not fully appreciate how good and great times were if I did not experience sad and awful times. We need the valleys to gauge the peaks. The level, constant monotony of settling and convenience crowds out the lows, but crowds out the highs as well. Pain, misery, suffering, and the storms of life really do provide us such a stark contrast with joy and peace. They help us appreciate the sunny side of life more.

When you think about it, life is a lot like summer in the South. There are long days of heat, humidity, and sun. It starts to wear on you. The ground starts to crack. The grass gets slightly less green. Then there is a real gully washer. The rain pours, trees fall, a trailer park gets eradicated, and everybody wants the sun back. When it comes back, the cracks in the ground are gone, the grass is green again, and everybody lends a hand getting the washing machine out of the tree.

Suffering is part of life. If we get rid of it, I am not so sure we will be able to say we are living anymore.

# THREE

# FROM JACKSON TO DUBAI
*Seeing the World Changes You*

I would not be who I am but for my time away from the United States. The decade I lived abroad as a child shaped me and defined me. Others are often surprised to learn I lived overseas for so long. I went from a small town to the world and back. Travel and life abroad have shaped my views on the world. My children will probably never have all the experiences around the world I had, but they will be shaped by how those experiences shaped me.

Jackson, Louisiana, is a town of four thousand people. I am pretty sure that number includes the people in the insane asylum. My family's house, called "the Bride's House" because it was built by the local fire marshal for his wife sometime after the Civil War, was only a few blocks from the asylum's fence. The bride, by the way, never lived in our house. She got sucked out the window of her plantation home by a tornado.

My dad, if you believed his dad—and that was a big if—was the fifteenth in an unbroken chain of sixteen Erick Ericksons, and worked as a production foreman for an oil company. When I was five, his bosses told him we could either move overseas or he could find a new job.

I am now forty-one years old. I have been to twenty-two U.S. states in my life. By the time I was fifteen, after almost ten years of living in the United Arab Emirates, I had been to twenty-one countries. I have now been to twenty-seven. I do not know that Gunnar and Evelyn will get the opportunity to travel that much internationally, but I am insistent they get passports and travel some.

Moving to Dubai in 1981 was hard to process as a kid. The idea of moving halfway around the world seemed more fantasy than real. I remember telling kids at school in Jackson. No one seemed to understand it. I was not even anxious about leaving my friends, because it just seemed too surreal to believe. Movers would come to our home and load up our furniture for indefinite storage. My parents and grandmother worked frantically to divide our household items into necessities and nonessentials. The necessities would be shipped to Dubai by air and arrive two weeks later. The nonessentials would go by boat and arrive months later.

The day of our journey began with my grandparents and my mother's aunt Clara and uncle Edwin driving with us to New Orleans. We stayed by the airport in a Holiday Inn to await our early morning flight to Houston. It was in that hotel that I met the first true love of my life. As we ate dinner in the hotel restaurant, the most beautiful woman I had ever seen in my five years of life played the piano. Her long brown hair flowing, she expertly made her way through Bach, Beethoven, and Mozart. Watching her play was hypnotic.

At some point my father realized I had fallen in love with this goddess of music. I had rested my elbow on the restaurant table, my face in my hand, and stared, fixated as she moved across the keys. Unbeknownst to me, my elbow had come to reside in a pile of ketchup on my plate. The whole situation—an incident that to this day comes up at inconvenient moments thanks to my father's unyielding memory and ability to embarrass me in front of my children—came crashing down not with the realization that my elbow had sank into ketchup, but that my muse was actually an animatronic mannequin. Our relationship was not to be, just like my childhood in America.

At the Houston airport, we boarded a 747 for the first time. It was massive. Thanks to my dad's company, we were in first class, and my sisters and I used the privilege of youth and first-class travel to roam the plane as explorers. I still remember soaring above the clouds that first time. The jet roared forward from the runway, my ears began to pop, my sister Gretchen grabbed my hand and began squeezing the life out of it, the nose went up, and soon the quilt of land spread out beneath us intermixed with floating mashed potatoes.

Hours and multiple repeats of the *Muppets' Greatest Hits* later, we landed in the darkness of the Netherlands and were whisked off to a hotel with our army of luggage. None of us had ever experienced jet lag before and we managed to sleep through the day in Amsterdam. I was convinced the sun never rose there unless you were at the airport.

After resting, we returned to Schiphol Airport, boarded another 747, and flew off to our new home. A few hours before sunup, our plane landed in Dubai. As we walked off the plane, down a staircase to waiting buses, we prepared for the blast of heat. Instead, it was cold. Novembers in the Middle East get cold and rainy—our first cultural surprise.

I remember taking a pile of cassette tapes and a Walkman in my carry-on bag, along with my Bible. When the bus pulled up to the entryway at the airport, we were met by a guide who advised us to take our Bibles out and carry them in our hands lest they disappear going through customs. We made our way through customs and back out into the chilly air of the night, loaded our belongings into a van, and went off to the Metropolitan Hotel, at the time an institution in Dubai. Then, thankfully, we slept.

Our first morning in Dubai is one of the most vivid memories in my life. We had arrived in darkness in a foreign country with close to a dozen suitcases between the five of us—my parents, my two sisters, and me. Our two rooms were cramped, which forced us to spend most of our time out of the hotel room. On that first morning, we woke up and looked out the window, and for miles and miles all we could see was sand. The hills were sand dunes. Grass had been replaced by small, spindly shrubs the local Americans called camel grass. There were no clouds, just yellow waves of sand ascending to ever-darker blue.

We headed to breakfast convinced our meal would be exotic and terrible—perhaps they ate camel for breakfast. Leaving our hotel room, I looked out a giant window by the elevator—and the brown and yellow sand moved! I can remember it so distinctly. Was the sand alive? Then I realized it was a camel, but not just one camel. It was a whole herd. They were eating the camel grass outside the hotel. I stared. My sisters stared. This was now our home. Like Dorothy realizing she was not in Kansas anymore, we were not in Louisiana anymore.

Breakfast in the hotel was vastly more Western than any of us expected. We had our choice of pastries, eggs, and even bacon in a Muslim country. The children's menu had a few unusual items on it. I ordered one of them. The hotel and its Disney-themed children's menu called it Pinocchio Toast, which was the highly exotic meal of SpaghettiOs on toast. Thirty-six years later, I still eat this delicacy. Don't judge me.

After a week in the hotel, we moved to our home at 126 Sheikh Rashid Villa. Our phone number was 440955. All of this, even to a five-year-old kid, was bizarre. Though we had a garage with a door that had to be manually raised and lowered, the home had no heating, and there was a high wall around the home flanked by towering eucalyptus and almond trees. The roof was flat. My dad and I could climb up top and camp out on it.

The left side of the house and backyard were desert. The front yard and right side of the house had grass planted. There was an empty servant's quarters in the back, a two-room cube. The smaller room served as a kitchen and bathroom combined. The shower was both a toilet and shower. I had never seen anything like it. None of us had.

We were on the corner of a row of houses that all looked the same. All these years later, only my house remains. The rest have been leveled. Like everything else in a desert, the sands and progress shift away old things. Being on the corner gave us a larger yard, three bedrooms, two and a half bathrooms, and a screened-in front porch. Though not gated, the three blocks surrounding us were mostly American families who worked for my dad's company. Our next-door neighbors were from Longview, Texas. The people across the street were from Houston. Our school was walking distance down the street. We really would be walking to school in desert heat, though at the time the concept of desert heat was still foreign to us.

Our house had three bedrooms and a TV room. Liefje, my oldest sister, got a room. Gretchen, my middle sister, and I were to share a room. That arrangement lasted twenty-four hours, at which point I claimed the TV room as my bedroom. That was all well and good, except I would have to deal with people in my room watching TV. This was a perfectly acceptable solution, which turned awesome as Liefje grew up and went away to boarding school, then back to the United States for high school. She would come home and let me stay up late watching *21 Jump Street* and other questionably appropriate shows with her.

November through March in Dubai is the rainy season. As the temperatures dropped, the rain began. The temperature could get down into the forties at night and into the seventies during the day. It was pleasant until April. Temperatures would begin the steady climb above 110. We learned there were days we could dry clothes faster hanging them in the backyard than running them through a dryer.

School, too, was an adventure. Liefje would start in seventh grade. Gretchen would go into third grade. I would go into first grade with Miss Sarah Brown. My oldest sister and I were the shy kids. My middle sister was the extrovert. Making friends never came easy, but I entered a class of similarly situated students.

The various American oil companies in Dubai had founded the Jumeirah American School. My dad's company, the Dubai Petroleum Company, played a key role and most of its employees' children attended. It was and remains one of the best schools in the world. My first-grade class had students from the United States, Canada, Sweden, Britain, Pakistan, India, Hong Kong, Sri Lanka, Australia, and more. Nine years later, as I prepared to depart Dubai, only one of my first-grade classmates would still be there.

I do not even know where most of my friends from elementary school are now. For some of them I cannot even remember their names without scrolling through yearbooks. But I remember the teachers. The teachers were the best.

The Dubai of then is not the Dubai of today. The Dubai of 1981 was a Dubai without a golf course. Its tallest building and only real skyscraper was, at the time, the tallest in the Middle East, at thirty-nine stories. Now that building is a midget among giants. But as it does now, Dubai had just about the best of everything. If you wanted authentic Mexican food, you could find it. Indian food? They had the best. Chinese food was amazing. There were even liquor stores for the Westerners in Dubai.

Long before most Americans had experience with farmers' markets, we could go to the market in Dubai to get fish right off the boat, spices, herbs, vegetables—just about anything. Thinking about it, my mouth waters. The smells of curry, cinnamon, clove, garlic, coriander—they float through the air. They are the smells of childhood and my youth. I can picture in my head the barrels and burlap sacks of spices. I can see the women with henna on their arms. I remember the shops filled with gold in the souk.

Dubai in the 1980s was a more innocent place than now. I have not been back since we left before the First Gulf War, but my friends who have gone back hate it. They say it is commercial and overgrown. The old buildings have been bulldozed for new and shiny. History has given way to modernity. It is the cosmopolitan version of Ozymandias.

As a kid growing up in Dubai, I could not have had a better life. The whole city was our playground. We could go just a few miles into the desert to camp and watch the Milky Way. My friends and I would stay up all night roaming our neighborhood, checking in only occasionally with our parents. On Saturdays, the football field at our school would get watered with high-powered sprinklers. We would all meet at sunup and run around the field waiting for the sprinkler heads to pop out of the ground and knock us over with a jet of water. We could walk the few blocks to the beach and swim or go to my dad's office, with its Olympic-size swimming pool. We could take taxis into Deira to the souks and spice markets and go shopping in Satwa, which had every counterfeit item of clothing imaginable. I tell Christy stories now of growing up there and she is mildly horrified by the free-range nature of being a kid there.

On the weekends, my mother would go to the hypermarket to shop. The downstairs had groceries and the upstairs had toys, furniture, etc. The American kids would go upstairs and play with the toys, only to be chased out by the owner's son. Years later I would attend Mercer University and wanted to take an international politics course my freshman year. Given my background, it seemed a natural fit. I had to go speak with the head of the political science department. I explained that I had grown up overseas and been to more countries than states. He was quite intrigued by my growing up in Dubai. "Did you know of the hypermarket?" he asked.

"Yes," I said. "I used to go in there with my friends while our parents shopped and play with the toys. We were always getting chased out of there by the owner's son. How do you know it?"

"I was the owner's son," he said, and smiled. Small world.

During the eighties, Dubai had the major dry dock in the Persian Gulf. The U.S. Navy would come into Dubai for repairs and maintenance and my parents volunteered to host parties for the enlisted sailors. My dad would cook ribs and buy lots of beer. My mom would organize the neighbors and run car pools, do laundry, and keep a stock of cigarettes for the sailors in our nonsmoking house. We had sailors come through from dozens of ships.

In March 1986, President Reagan sent U.S. warships to engage Libya in the Gulf of Sidra. The USS *Richmond K. Turner* participated in the engagement and soon after happened into dry docks in Dubai. We entertained the crew right around my birthday and the captain gave me shell casings from the ship that he said came from the engagement. It was a great birthday present and I still have them on my desk. The *Coronado*, *Vincennes*, *La Salle*, and numerous other ships saw their sailors in and out of our home.

Most notably, after the USS *Samuel B. Roberts* hit a mine in the Persian Gulf and hobbled into Dubai, my parents adopted many of those sailors as family. I would wake up some mornings and be surrounded by sailors sleeping on the floor. For months my parents and our neighbors served as surrogate families for the sailors. We fed them, took them shopping, went with them to the beach, and had fun. They were like big brothers. It is no surprise my oldest sister wound up marrying a sailor.

Entertaining the navy gave my entire family a strong sense of patriotism to a nation, despite being halfway around the world. The American flag kept us and the world safe. People relied on it and understood it had meaning beyond just another country. Sometimes it caused trouble. On more than one occasion our school was shut down due to bomb threats. Our school would take the sixth-grade class on a trip to Kenya and the ninth-grade class could select a place to go for a "senior" class trip. For a time these trips stopped. Occasionally, we would have armed guards at the gates of our school digging through our sandwiches to check for explosives. I remember my mom telling me that if anyone asked, I should say I was Swedish. With a name like Erickson, it was plausible.

Our first year in Dubai came with our first fake Christmas tree and lots of Star Wars figures for me. Only a few months later we took our first trip abroad to renew our visas. My mother wanted to go to Cyprus, so we did. There we befriended a taxi driver named George, who lived with his sister in the mountains, herding goats and making cheese. He drove us all over the Greek part of Cyprus. From Nicosia to Larnaca to Limassol we saw castles, ruins, foundational bits of Greek mythology . . . and I nearly drowned. The rest of my family still laughs about this, but they were not in the water. We had got up into the mountains and there was an icy-cold stream flowing down. I got the bright idea of climbing up the rocks ever higher up the mountainside, until at some point I fell. I could not grab hold of the rocks to get out, because they were so slippery. I began to scream that I was drowning. My dad ran over and yanked me up. The water did not quite even come up to my knees. But I swear I was drowning. No one else believes me, though.

We spent a great deal of time in Penang, which to this day is my idea of paradise. It was a small island off the coast of Malaysia. We went at least five times. I taught myself to swim in the beachside pool of a Holiday Inn. My dad and I would rent a boat every time and have the boat captain take us to a secluded place called Monkey Beach, where we would fish. It was the only place I could remember being able to see straight down to the bottom of the sea. Everything about Penang was amazing. The Chinese and Malay food were exceptional, the people friendly, and the place so innocent.

One year, as we were flying home from Malaysia, the plane developed engine problems upon takeoff. The pilots had to make an emergency landing and we were stuck in Kuala Lumpur. Due to an international event, the city's hotels were completely booked. The Crowne Plaza hotel in Kuala Lumpur had just two available rooms. They just happened to be on the floor wholly reserved for President Zia of Pakistan. Thankfully, President Zia loved Ronald Reagan and was glad to host a stranded American family. I barely remember him, other than that he was quite nice, praised President Reagan, and insisted my sisters and I eat the Toblerone bars in the mini-fridge. That was our only encounter with him. A few years later he and the U.S. ambassador to Pakistan were assassinated.

We spent a great deal of time in Europe growing up. My parents had friends in Belgium, Germany, and Great Britain. We would take train rides through the Alps, eat chocolate in Switzerland, and tour the cathedrals of Germany. Every summer we would return home to the United States for a few months. Often we would go ahead of my dad, who would always have to stay behind a few weeks for work. One year, when I was eleven, the rest of the family decided they wanted to stay and wait for my dad, but I really wanted to get back to my grandparents. It was, at that time, a pretty natural thing to let kids fly home alone. My parents let me. They took me to the airport, loaded me on a KLM 747, and off I went.

Somewhere over the Black Sea the airplane developed severe mechanical problems. The plane had to make a very hard and rough emergency landing in Innsbruck, Austria. My French teacher, Mrs. Gwydir, was on the plane with her family, but otherwise I knew not a soul on board. For hours we sat in Innsbruck Airport until a DC-10 from Lauda Air could be procured to get us all to Amsterdam. We finally made it to Amsterdam, but in the chaos I lost my KLM chaperone. However, I knew where I was going. I had been doing this for years. I hustled to the next gate and arrived just as they were closing the door of the KLM flight to Atlanta. The agent at the gate stared at me incredulously. "You cannot board. The gate is closed and you do not have your parents," she told me. I really wanted to cry. Instead I raised my hand, pulled my sleeve, and revealed the unaccompanied-minor bracelet I was wearing. The poor lady turned ghost white, picked up a phone, and began rambling in Dutch at top speed.

The 747 pushed back from the gate. She turned, stared out the window, turned back to me, and talked even faster and louder. She put down the phone, looked at me, and told me to have a seat. Another lady from KLM soon came up to me and apologized repeatedly. She informed me that my parents would be notified, I would be booked on the next flight to Atlanta, and they would arrange for me to stay in a hotel overnight because the next flight would not be until the following day. There was just one more catch. The Jehovah's Witnesses were having an international conference near the airport and the closest hotel was in Amsterdam.

The lady escorted me to a van, placed my luggage in the van, then told me goodbye. I was driven to downtown Amsterdam, right by the red-light district, to a hotel where I promptly went to sleep. Sometime during the night I awoke to two hotel employees entering the room to try to get it on. My screaming ran them off. The next morning, a driver returned me to the airport, where a chaperone escorted me to first class on a 747 headed to Atlanta. Upon arrival, I believe every person my parents knew on the eastern seaboard of the United States met me to make sure I had all my fingers and toes. Once I had survived that ordeal, my parents never again hesitated to let me travel alone.

To this day, I love to travel, though I do it so much less than before. I long to take Gunnar, Evelyn, and Christy to London, Paris, and Munich. I want to take them to Dubai. But traveling abroad is an expense we cannot afford, with medical bills and student loans. It was great when my dad's company paid for it all. Not so much when I have to pay for it. Whether we are able to travel abroad later in their childhoods, or my children do it in college or young adulthood on their own, I want them to go.

In the meantime, we will travel the country and see places I have never seen as we build memories with them and their mom. As a kid, when we would come home during the summer, my dad would rent the biggest car he could, often a Cadillac. We would pile in and drive all over to see his family, who were more spread out than my mom's. We would drive through North Carolina to see an old friend of his en route to South Carolina. We would stay on a mountaintop in South Carolina at my aunt Lela's, then drive to Eustis, Florida, to my aunt LaVerne's.

My sisters and I would spread out across the back of the car, piles of tapes for our Walkmans, Mad Lib books, and cameras. We would endure the misery of long road trips for the excitement of seeing familiar places and family.

Seeing the world and the nation up close gives us a greater appreciation for both the community we have around us and how interconnected so many communities are. We are not isolated in the world. High walls do nothing except prevent exchanges of ideas and people. The world looks on our nation in wonder. We have obligations to the world that we helped forge after the Second World War. We cannot withdraw. If we do, others will stand up who do not share our values or the values of our liberal democracy.

I have seen the poorest of the poor begging in the streets of India. I have seen the richest of the rich in their Arabian palaces and Hollywood mansions. There is so much different between them, but they all have aspirations, hopes, worries, fears, and dread. They all want something more. So many of them look to our nation as a land of wonder and opportunity. We have much to be thankful for. Much is expected of those who have been given much, and our nation has been given a great deal. Traveling the world changes you, but it can also inspire you to change the world right back.

# • FOUR •
# YALLA, HABIBI, AND SHWAY SHWAY

*Those Around You Shape You*

Gunnar and Evelyn are going to be shaped by Christy and me, but I am mindful that it is not just their parents they will learn from. They will pick up habits and knowledge from friends, teachers, and others. I would not be who I am but for the work of others. Drawing lines between individuality and community can be hard. We are all unique individuals, but none of us should ever forget those who helped shape us. I value the worth of the individual more than the community, but after all, it is a collection of individuals who form the community and give it character. That community's character and the character of other individuals in turn shape our character.

When I look back on my life, I see the bits and pieces others have contributed to the quilt of my own character.

As a third grader attending Jumeirah American School in Dubai, I was taught by a woman named Helen Bruskas, a fiery Greek who made the best chocolate chip pound cake to ever exist on the planet. Short of funerals in the South, third-grade birthdays in Dubai were the only time I would get pound cake. Mrs. Bruskas would make one for each student in her class who had a birthday. All the third graders were scared to death of Mrs. Bruskas. She was exacting and brusque. But we loved her at the same time. If she said "jump" in her thick Greek accent, none of us would ask how high. We would just know she expected us to jump as high as we could. For her, we would do anything. If we did not, we knew that Greek temper would be forthcoming.

Mrs. Bruskas had a pure love for literature. Every school day she expected us to read and write. For Mrs. Bruskas, these simple tasks were something extra. We had to write creatively, we had to read silently and be able to prove we understood what we had read, and then we had to do it some more.

Gunnar and Evelyn will, I hope, appreciate all their teachers. But I hope they really treasure the great ones. There are a lot of good teachers. But only a few are great enough to shape lives. Mrs. Bruskas was one of those.

Every day before lunch, we would sit in a circle and Mrs. Bruskas would play a record of someone singing the multiplication tables. We were expected to sing along. Failure to sing along meant no recess. No recess meant having to stay in the classroom with Mrs. Bruskas. We may have all loved her, but giving up recess to sit in a classroom was for years the closest thing I could imagine to purgatory.

You never wanted to engage Mrs. Bruskas in a conversation if you had to stay in at recess. If you fell for her trick, you might answer a seemingly innocent question of hers by telling her about things you had done, places you had been, and experiences you'd had. Then she would wonder aloud why you had not written about those things in your creative papers.

This inevitably led to more work. We could skate by with short pieces if Mrs. Bruskas did not know all the details. But if anyone fell for her trick, suddenly five paragraphs about a trip to India or Hong Kong became five pages. She expected details. She expected quality from her third graders.

On Fridays, on the way to recess, everyone had to pass by Mrs. Bruskas at a side door to the classroom. To get past her, we all had to be able to sing the multiplication table of the week. If you messed up, you stayed inside. For twelve weeks of school this went on. Then, if that was not enough torture, we had to figure out division.

Mrs. Bruskas made us write, and in time, our writing improved. Slowly she taught us how to diagram sentences. From diagramming sentences, she made us go back through everything we had written and improve it. Thirty-four years later, my palms still sweat thinking about it all.

I remember one story I wrote about a whale. The whale was blue and blew water out of its spout. The whale had been hunted by fishermen, but the whale hid underwater, holding its breath. But the fishermen waited. The whale needed to surface for air. It rose to the surface under the boat and blew water out of its spout, lifting the boat into the air. My story was on large lined grade school paper. It was stapled across the top and affixed to a drawing I had made of the whale with the spray coming from its spout.

That would be a simple story, except nothing was that simple for an exacting taskmaster like Mrs. Bruskas. Why, she wondered, was the whale blue? A blue whale is not very original. It could have been a killer whale, sleek and black. What happened to the fishermen and the boat? What happened to them after the water ran out and the boat crashed down? Why did they give up the hunt?

Here I was, a third grader proud of a hand-drawn whale with a story attached in my best handwriting. Still, Mrs. Bruskas wanted me to think harder, be more original, and understand that good stories should offer satisfying endings and answer unresolved questions. Looking back on this now, it is remarkable that a teacher would expect so much from a third grader. But what is more remarkable is that so many of Mrs. Bruskas's students rose to her challenge.

Our stories would become more detailed, more vivid, and more original. Our illustrations, too. The whale would become rare, yellow—hunted for being extraordinary. The ship would sink and the whale would rescue the fishermen to finally make peace. Mrs. Bruskas pushed us in extraordinary ways—in ways I am not sure people expect teachers to push third-grade students now.

She showed so many of us what could be. She opened our heads to wonder. She made us understand that passable and acceptable were at the bottom end of the scale. She also made sure we knew that we could fall flat on our face and she would help us back up, but we had to learn a lesson. We had to know why we failed, why we fell, why we came up short. I became a writer in Mrs. Bruskas's third-grade classroom.

Third grade also brought me my one and only encounter with Mrs. Wahabi, who affects Evelyn's and Gunnar's lives more than they or Mrs. Wahabi could ever know. She taught Arabic Culture and had no sense of humor. "Yalla, yalla!" she would yell. "Yalla habibi!" That was for us to hurry. "Shway, shway!" was when she wanted us to slow down or be quiet. I remember the pillars of Islam. I remember how to write my name in Arabic. I remember the tourist words for hello, goodbye, thank you, and good to meet you. I also remember that *dajajah* is chicken.

Gunnar and Evelyn find no humor in my repeated attempts to take them to "Dajajah-fil-A," nor do they appreciate when I yell at them in Arabic to hurry or slow down. "Yalla!" is the morning cry to get a move on for school. But I make sure to smile. One teacher, from a single class I took thirty years ago, left enough of an impression on me that I yell at my kids in Arabic in the grocery store.

If Mrs. Bruskas set me on the path, Mr. Middlebrook put the spotlight on it. Mr. Middlebrook was one of the most multitalented people I have ever encountered. He shaped me probably more than any other teacher I have ever had. You know how sometimes you pick up a hobby or an interest and only later you realize you did it because you observed someone else enjoying it so much? That is Stephen Middlebrook to me.

My first encounter with Mr. Middlebrook was in fourth grade. He was my music teacher. Every kid had to learn to play the recorder. But we did not just have to learn to play the recorder. We also had to learn about composers. It was mighty easy to put fingers on a stick and blow. But to put fingers on a stick, blow, and understand that behind those sounds were legends with names like Beethoven, Mozart, Bach, Brahms, Chopin, and Bizet was something else entirely.

Mr. Middlebrook would regale us with tales of

the child prodigy Mozart. Beethoven's father beat him because he wanted him to be like Mozart. Beethoven composed symphonies while deaf. If he could do that, what could we do? We had to be silent. We had to listen. We had to appreciate music. Mr. Middlebrook would tell us we did not have to like particular music, but we at least needed to understand why it was significant. Did I mention this was fourth grade? I loved that class.

I can picture Mr. Middlebrook's class still. The walls were covered in bulletin boards. Our chairs were in a circle. He would start each class with the biography of a composer. Our job was to linger on his words and memorize facts about these men. Then we would play. Leading a group of fourth graders playing recorders requires the patience of Job and the sense of humor of Bozo the Clown, both of which Mr. Middlebrook possessed. He could laugh off anything. I do not recall ever seeing him angry. And I still play my recorder.

When Evelyn entered fourth grade a few years ago, she had to learn the recorder, too. I went online and found the exact same music lesson book Mr. Middlebrook used with us thirty-three years earlier. I can picture him now doing as I did with Evelyn, seated, stomping his feet back and forth, singing along to the tune.

"The grand old Duke of York / He had ten

thousand men / He marched them up to the top of the hill / And he marched them down again."

After passing through fifth grade, where my teacher was Mrs. Bruskas's husband, Spiro, I would arrive at what is still my favorite grade, sixth. Sixth grade at the Jumeirah American School involved ancient history. The teachers, Mr. Middlebrook and Miss Long, decided to build the entire year around the Greeks. Mr. Middlebrook seemingly knew everything about Greek and Roman mythology, architecture, history—you name it. For a year, I ate, drank, and slept with Greek myths. Doric, Ionic, and Corinthian columns were in my dreams.

Mr. Middlebrook rewrote Aristophanes's *The Birds*. Every sixth grader had a part. Along the way, we had to learn about Greek tragedy and comedy. We had to learn about amphitheaters. So obsessed was he with us getting it right, at one point when the school upgraded its playgrounds, Mr. Middlebrook convinced the administration to install an acoustically correct mini-amphitheater. It was not much to look at, but drop a pin in the center and no matter where you sat, you could hear it hit the ground perfectly.

Like Mrs. Bruskas, Mr. Middlebrook made us write and write and write some more. One of my most valuable lessons in writing came from my spectacular failure in trying to impress Mr. Middlebrook.

We had read *Bridge to Terabithia*, a wonderful

but sad tale about a boy and girl who create an imaginary kingdom in the forest where they escape from bullies and rule as absolute monarchs until one of the children dies. After reading it, we had to write our own true-life adventure tales. We would write a first draft, Mr. Middlebrook would then give us notes, then we would do a final draft. My adventure centered on exploring the forest behind my grandparents' home back in Louisiana. Back there along the bayou and gullies, my friend Ryan and I had discovered a collapsed bridge and ruins. Our discovery was pretty cool in itself. But to impress Mr. Middlebrook, I embellished some aspects of my story. Ryan and I were on a raft, we floated down the river and nearly drowned, the roof of the old mansion nearly collapsed on us. It was spectacular. Had I killed off Ryan at the end of it, I am certain I could have gotten a Newbery Medal.

Mr. Middlebrook was having none of it. He did not even make it past the second page. There were five more college-ruled loose-leaf notebook pages of my eight-point-type handwriting to go. He had not even gotten to the part with the snake. He truly would have been dazzled. But he could spot crap from a mile away.

He never called me out. He never embarrassed me in front of other people. He just penned in red, "No. Tell me your story, not your imagined story. Start over." He never said a word.

Embarrassed by getting called out on my fiction, I tried to remember the experience more deeply. The forest that surrounded my grandparents' home on two sides held many secrets and it was largely impenetrable due to erosion. It was bordered by a deep gulley, through which a creek flowed. There was virtually no way down to that creek. One day, hacking through underbrush with a five-foot-long steel pipe a plumber had left behind at my grandparents' house, Ryan and I discovered a smooth sloping path leading down to the creek.

At creek level, Ryan and I discovered that we could walk along the banks of the creek and make it around behind my grandparents' home down the cliff that served as my grandparents' personal garbage dump. We found the remains of an old home. There was what appeared to be an old wooden bridge. Some of the beams still existed, but the frame of the house had long since burned down. Everything was covered in vines.

Ryan saw a snake. We hated snakes and both suddenly came to the realization that if there was one snake, there were probably others. So we ran, making our escape through thick brush and thorns. By the time we reached my grandparents' house again, we were scraped and bloodied—but we'd had an adventure.

I wrote that story, just the facts. Five pages grew into eight pages. There were details of smells and sounds. The rustle of leaves underfoot gave way to the sounds of running water. It was all there in vivid detail and this time all of it was true. I bound it in oversize green construction paper and drew cover artwork.

Not only did Mr. Middlebrook like it, but I got the highest grade in the class. He let everybody know how well I had written. For a fleeting moment, I felt real pride in myself. He told me afterward that the truth would be the only thing anyone would ever want of me. He said that when people write fiction, they weave in truths the readers are meant to grasp. Deep down we all want truth, even in imagined stories, fables, and legends. Even today, when writing and talking about politics and the news, this lesson echoes in my brain.

Our theatrical production of *The Birds*, an ancient Greek comedy, had truths in it, too. It was also a lot of work. I was a woodpecker. I was not good enough to be one of the main characters— Optimistes and Obstinatos. The names may not have been the same as the original, but the basic plot points were the same.

We sixth graders all put on our mothers' pantyhose, hopped into overstuffed bird costumes local tailors had made, and prepared for our roles. "Woodpeckers, woodpeckers, sharpen up your beaks. Everybody quiet while the partridge speaks." I can remember that line after all these years. My friend James had the coolest line of the play, though. He was the vulture. "Some birds say drop in. Other birds say drop by. We vultures say drop dead." To this day, whenever I see a vulture eating roadkill on a South Georgia highway, I recite that line without fail.

Mr. Middlebrook went on to become the principal at the Jumeirah American School. He also encouraged the school to move from the Apple II series computer to the Macintosh. He had a Mac SE/30 in his office. We're talking 1 megabyte of RAM and an 80-megabyte hard drive. Using the Mac platform and the Apple IIGS, Mr. Middlebrook launched a class on desktop publishing for the junior high school. The class would churn out a school newspaper of sorts.

Evelyn and Gunnar groan whenever I quote that vulture line and whenever I start critiquing fonts on signs and packaging. I tell them they have to blame Mr. Middlebrook. I am, because of him, a font snob. I learned kerning and the basics of typography from him. Though he only taught us the differences between serif and sans serif fonts, I dove deeper into a passion for fonts, eventually going so far as to learn the differences between Helvetica and Arial, the latter of which is far inferior.

Mr. Ackerman ran the school's computer lab and taught programming. Mr. Ackerman was also my advisor in ninth grade, and basically served as a homeroom teacher. He let me run the school's computer lab in the afternoon. Having no computer at home, I was there most days anyway, if only to play Oregon Trail and mess around in Print Shop. Mr. Ackerman pushed the school to embrace computers, not a given back then. Even in first grade we had an Apple II computer. In fourth grade, typing was a required class before Mavis Beacon had even started teaching it. We also were required to take Logo computer programming that year. (Side note: Only now as I am writing this book did I learn that Mavis Beacon is not a real person! Part of my childhood just died.)

My most striking memory of Mr. Ackerman and the one that probably had the most impact on me is one that only involved him indirectly. I had gotten a C on a project in science class. It seems like such a small thing now. I cannot even remember all the details. When Mr. Radtke, the science teacher, had told me I could do the project over, I was indignant. I remember I had worked my butt off and had gotten approval each step of the way and encouragement about the direction I was going. I had been floored by the bad grade when the project came back.

In the notes on my report card, the teacher noted that I could have done the project again, but had refused. During a conference with my parents, Mr. Ackerman asked me why I did not redo the project. I explained I had done it while getting approval and good feedback each step of the way and had no expectation that it would turn out differently, given the circumstances. I thought the grade was simply unfair.

Mr. Ackerman let out a big smile on his face and just said, "Well, at least you are honest and thought about it." Then he turned to my parents and said, "If that's the case and he thinks he did his best, there is no reason for you to be upset." Not only did it get me out of trouble, but it was the first time I really remember an authority figure siding with me, a kid, instead of the adult. Even now, when Evelyn and Gunnar have problems with adults at school, I remember Mr. Ackerman's willingness to believe me instead of defaulting to just accepting another adult's assessment at face value. I also went on to make a B in that science class after figuring out that water can only be sucked up a straw so high before air pressure and vacuum collide into the weight of the column of the water.

Mr. Radtke may have disagreed with me on my project, but he instilled in me a love of chemistry. In Dubai in the eighties, one did not need a license to buy chemicals. I would get tips on cool science experiments from Mr. Radtke and go buy the chemicals in bulk. I was probably the only kid in school with a two-liter bottle of hydrochloric acid in his pantry. I would drop zinc into a flask, pour in the HCl, and fill balloons with hydrogen to then set matches to. On Saturdays, my backyard was like Naval Air Station Lakehurst when the *Hindenburg* exploded.

I am kind of surprised I never got killed. Having sufficiently exploded hydrogen, Mr. Radtke encouraged me to up my game with hydrogen peroxide and potassium permanganate to release oxygen for ignition. For the longest time, I wanted to be a chemist. Unfortunately, it all came to an end when I had to dump my homemade chemistry set upon leaving Dubai. Most of the chemicals were in liquid form and no shipping company would let me pack them. Instead, I invited over friends and we blew up my backyard. The coup de grâce was igniting the small piece of potassium Mr. Radtke had given me for the occasion. Replicating my favorite experiment of his, I put phenolphthalein in water, then dumped in the chunk of potassium. The water boiled, turned a bright pink, and exploded. It was awesome.

Two weeks before I finished writing this book, Mr. Ackerman died. My sister sent me a notice she had seen on Facebook. I had not seen the man since I was in ninth grade. But I cannot sit in front of a computer without thinking about him. When Evelyn and Gunnar talk about homeroom teachers, I think about Mr. Ackerman standing up for me. When the kids want a new app for the iPad, I think about Mr. Ackerman letting me help decide what software to buy for school and letting me try it out first on the Apple IIGS. I think about his insistence that I learn Logo computer programming in fourth grade and BASIC programming in 1987. "It's the future and it'll make you smart," he would say.

It is funny how all these things, learned at an early age, somehow influence you later in life. I may never need to do a quadratic equation again, but white space, fonts, and design come back to me often. When Evelyn and Gunnar question why they are learning something in school, I tell them that they may never use it, but then again, they might find later on in life that they do use it, and more than they would think.

When I moved back to Louisiana in 1990, Saddam Hussein was on the verge of invading Kuwait. My whole family repatriated and my dad continued flying back and forth every twenty-eight days. We actually knew the Gulf War had started because my dad was flying into Dubai. We knew when he should have landed. He always called. But he did not. Several hours went by before we heard from him. Something had to have happened. My mom offhandedly said, "I guess we've invaded Iraq." A short time later, NBC's Tom Brokaw came on the news to announce the Gulf War had begun. Then my dad called. He said his plane had been diverted and landed late.

Gas prices spiked over $1.25 because of the war. My parents had enrolled me in the Wilkinson County Christian Academy in Woodville, Mississippi, when we returned home. I had a thirty-minute drive each way. When gas was $0.79, it was no big deal. But once it got to the outrageous price of $1.25, they decided to move me to the public school a few miles from our house.

Culture shock set in. I had come from a school in the Middle East that had kids from all over the globe, then briefly attended a private school with nothing but white kids, and ended up in a multiracial public school in one of the poorest parishes of Louisiana. My first week of public school at Jackson High School was a nightmare. The students were disruptive, several of the teachers clearly were phoning it in, and I was grades ahead, but without the course credit. I had started taking French in seventh grade and had to enroll in a beginner's French class in tenth grade—a class with no textbooks, no less.

In Dubai, the teachers had a copy center. Students would carry over a teacher's work and within an hour or so we would all have crisp photocopied handouts. In Jackson, we had mimeograph machines. Everything was fuzzy and purple. In Dubai, we had state-of-the-art science equipment. In Jackson, the little equipment we had was kept under lock and key. In Dubai, we spoke the King's English. In Jackson, well, Elvis was from Memphis.

My first week I sat in an English class and a student raised his hand because he did not recognize a word. The word? *Liberty.* I would have been vastly angrier with my parents for sending me to this place had I not been in a constant state of disbelief. It made me appreciate so much more the education I had gotten in Dubai.

I finally met my match with Carla Boykin. She was having none of the "I've already had this class" excuse. Read *Silas Marner*? I was going to have to read it again and would be graded more precisely. Shakespeare? Why yes— how about an essay on the differences between Elizabeth Taylor's Cleopatra and Shakespeare's *Julius Caesar* and *Antony and Cleopatra*? A report? How about going to the college library at Louisiana State University (LSU) and using advanced resources? She pushed and pushed.

I did find one cheat in her class. Having been the only kid in school without a computer in Dubai, I became, for a short time, the only kid in school with a computer in Jackson. Eventually, several friends got them, too. But for a bright, shining moment, I had a custom-built, top-of-the-line 66Mhz computer with an 80Mhz hard drive running cutting-edge MS-DOS 4.01. I desperately wanted a Mac, but to no avail.

Mrs. Boykin let me type my spelling homework. She did not appreciate the power of WordPerfect, still today the best word processing program out there. With WordPerfect I could write a word once, copy it, and paste it the requisite four more times. Suddenly my English homework was a breeze. But that was the only cheat, and if I ever caught Gunnar and Evelyn doing it I'd put them back to pencil and paper in a heartbeat.

Mrs. Boykin set the standard for my high school public education. She had regular classes and honor classes. Those of us in the honor classes never had an easy time. But the challenge built camaraderie at a time when I had trouble making friends, and the work was never boring.

Dr. Scott, my chemistry and physics teacher, determined she would challenge me, too. She also gave me extra credit for going to see *Star Trek VI*. Mrs. Welch, in American History, would let me read the newspaper and talk politics. She was my one open Republican teacher and was pretty horrified when it looked like Bill Clinton would become president.

I had some horrible teachers, too. I barely remember them. They have no power over me and no part of them is embedded within me. But all of those people and events I mention here became and continue to be a part of me. I would not be doing what I am doing but for each of them. We are all a part of something greater than ourselves. Bits and pieces of us embed within the souls of others, helping shape their character. The negative can be as influential as the positive. The ability to experience new things, to see the world in a different way, and to be yelled at in Arabic all combine to shape our worldview and our character.

I am the man I am because of how my parents raised me and how others shaped me. None of them bear responsibility for me. My character is my own. I am as unique as every other person is unique. But the color of my eyes, my amazing ability to get sunburned just thinking about being outside, and my desire to go to Dajajah-fil-A all originated elsewhere. I cannot blame them for the bad. I must take responsibility as Evelyn and Gunnar must take responsibility for themselves. But I hope they will appreciate where the parts of their habits and personalities come from, and I hope, through this, they understand more about me and where my habits and personality come from.

# • FIVE •
# FORGIVENESS AND REGRET
## *The Importance of Letting Go*

My father's father lived well into his nineties, if not older. No one seemed completely sure what year the man was born in. Both my mother's parents lived into their nineties. My great-aunts and great-uncles in my mother's family survived into old age and most of my father's siblings lived a long time, too. With all the longevity in my family, the blood clots in my lungs threw me for a loop. I never thought I would have to worry about dying. I never expected I would need to write down lessons for my children. Life, however, is full of surprises.

One of the interesting side effects of growing up is realizing how young people see old people. I remember being a kid and thinking about how old my teachers and other adults were. It is like my house. When I was a kid, the house was huge. I remember sliding down the bannister from the second floor. I remember running down the long hallway, dropping to my knees, and sliding the rest of the way. I remember playing hide-and-seek and having so much room. But then we moved to Dubai, and when we returned home a decade later, the house did not feel that big anymore. After I went away to college and came home for that first Christmas, the house seemed like it had shrunk even further as I grew taller. The hallway was no longer long enough to slide down. The bannister was too low. The rooms were smaller and seemingly crammed with bigger furniture. As a child you latch on to perceptions of things. As an adult, you find yourself surprised by how different everything really is.

I am now older than the teachers I thought were so old when I was a kid. When I was a teenager, the idea of reaching my fifties or sixties seemed unfathomably remote. Now that I am in my forties, the seventies seem like the prime of life. In my seventies, if all goes according to plan, I can have more free time to travel. I am pretty sure I never want to retire. That seems to be when people die. But I should at least have a few months of vacation accumulated to be able to travel the world and go back to Dubai.

My children see people my age and wonder how long it will take them to get to that point in life. I see people older than me and wonder what it will be like when my children go to college. I wonder how Christy and I will have raised them, will they still want to do later what they want to do now, and I worry about them, our future, our finances—the wondering and worrying is normal and also silly. It will all be here before I know it and before they know it.

When I was a kid, I really wanted to grow up. It seemed so cool. When you grow up, you get a car. You get to drive. You have money. You can travel and buy cool stuff. What you do not realize is that it all comes with a price. There is no more summer vacation. There are debts and bills to be paid. The creeping soreness in your shoulders becomes chronic. You want to be a kid again. I tell Gunnar and Evelyn to enjoy it while they can, but I get the sense that right now, at eight and eleven, they do not really understand. They see kids older than themselves and think those kids have more freedom. They do not see that those kids' parents also have more worries. They see adults who have paychecks. They do not see the gray hair that comes with the stress. They do not have a concept of losing summer vacation. Even now, I work from home. During the summers they see me flow in and out of my office. They just think I am a workaholic, which I admit I am in part. But also, I have flexibility with my job. They do not really understand what it is like to have a parent gone all day to an office. They see me travel. I can often be gone for days on end. But when I am home, I am home. One day they will be in for a rude awakening. For now, I try to get them to enjoy their youth.

One of the terrible aspects of youth that never

goes away, however, is insult and injury. Life may be short, but insult and injury can bind to us, weigh us down, and never let go. Of all the lessons I want Gunnar and Evelyn to learn, I want them to learn to forgive and let go. For many people, it seems to be the hardest lesson. I do not know if people are hardwired to be able to forgive or hold on to things. I try always to forgive. As I have gotten older, and dumber, I have come to realize how much more I need forgiveness and how often people refuse to forgive. Even now, people will bring up something I did a decade or so ago. Social media is the worst in that respect. There is no grace and no forgiveness there. Everyone is bound by their former sins, no matter how often or how much they have apologized. I do not want Gunnar and Evelyn to be like that.

My wife can tell stories from her childhood in which someone did something wrong. As she speaks, she will often get worked up. You can hear her voice change as she goes through the details of an ancient sleight or bad experience. I am not sure I remember very many encounters in my life like that.

I can think of only one sleight like that that I have ever hung on to. When I was in second grade, there was a terrible brat in my class named Adam. My father's company in Dubai had a complex behind the office building for all the workers' families. There was a restaurant, a grill, tennis courts, and a giant, Olympic-size pool. I was swimming and playing some game with Adam. But one day as I tried to come up from underwater, Adam got on top of me, wrapped his legs around my head, and refused to let me get to the surface. I can remember the sensation of desperately needing to breathe and not being able to. I was flailing about and thankfully some adult jerked the little jerk out of the water. I emerged crying. I remember my mother yelling at Adam. Still today, whenever I am climbing out of a pool or see my kids surrounded by other kids at one, I think about Adam that day. I do not like for even my kids to be near me when I am getting out of a pool and I know it is from that incident.

When we do not let go of something and when we cannot forgive, we are letting another person control us. I often see people who cannot forgive and who hold on to what happened to them and I see people being controlled by the shadow of a former memory. An inability to move beyond it, to forgive the foe, will resurface and burden people, weighing them down. It wounds one's soul. I see it in friends of mine and people I know.

I worked with a man for a long time who grew up in the shadow of his demanding father. The father, a great success, expected his son to be even more successful. To challenge his son, he pushed him harder and harder. Nothing was ever good enough. Praise was rare. As a consequence, I saw that man's son do two things as an adult. First, he checked out of his own children's lives. So afraid of becoming like his father, he provided no structure and no guidance to his kids. He really ruined his kids' lives because he would not motivate them. Where his father taught him that nothing was ever good enough, he taught his kids that they only needed to do the bare minimum. His kids never had a sense of strong self-worth, and not because they were pushed too hard, but because they were not pushed at all. Second, in his own profession he became compulsive in his need for precision. He was harder on himself than anyone else could be, but also constantly angry at those around him. This was largely—and it does not take a psychoanalyst to figure it out— because of his unsure standing under his father. He had never forgiven his father for how his father had treated him. He let it hang over him. His father's treatment of him controlled him. He became a pitiable creature, unable to let go while desperate to let go.

I suspect most everyone has some issue with how their parents raised them. Everyone has a story. But what you do with that story or that feeling matters so much. My wife worked for a law firm where the senior partner died. He had been a workaholic. He always put work ahead of family and he did so because he had grown up poor and did not want his family to live in similar circumstances. He was never home. He never went to his children's Little League games. When he died, his children did not show up at his funeral. He had no relationship with them and they had no relationship with him. He was married to his office.

For a while, my own dad worked offshore on an oil platform. My mother would load us all into the family camper long before sunrise and we would drive my dad south toward the Louisiana coast to send him off. A year later we moved to Dubai and he continued this routine. He would be gone for seven days and home for seven days. In high school, he would be gone a month and return a month. I never resented my dad for being gone. I missed him. I was in high school before we really connected strongly. Still, I knew he did what he did for the family and so that I would not have to. He never demanded of me what he did and never expected me to follow in his footsteps. There was never any question of that. I hope to one day be half the man my father is and I know he expects me to be better than him.

I expect Gunnar and Evelyn to be better than me. Wanting our children to outdo us is one of life's goals for any parent. Part of that, however, is teaching your kids how to forgive you, because you are going to screw up. Parenting does not come with an instructions manual and most of those written to serve that purpose are pretty freaking terrible. You are going to screw up as a parent. How you handle the screwup will determine whether or not your kid grows up with daddy issues. Teaching forgiveness as a way to not let others have control is hard, but necessary.

I am reminded of the story of the crucifixion. Jesus of Nazareth got hauled into a show trial. The locals in Jerusalem who had welcomed him into the city a few days before by laying down palm branches now chanted "crucify him." Pilate offered up either Jesus or a murderer for release and the people chose the murderer for release. Jesus was savagely beaten—beaten so badly that his flesh and bone were exposed. The Roman soldiers put a crown of thorns on his head that cut into his scalp. So weakened by the beating, someone had to help Jesus carry his own cross to his crucifixion. Then the soldiers nailed him to the cross and lifted it. His body and gravity pulled on the nails in his flesh. Still, he forgave the people. Think about that as a picture of forgiveness. If you are unwilling to forgive someone, you are really saying your conscience is more afflicted than Jesus's conscience. You are saying that the innocent man nailed to the cross for the sins of others was not as wronged as you. Do you really want to do that? If Jesus could forgive, surely you and I can forgive.

The corollary to forgiveness of others is that

sometimes you have to forgive yourself. Regret can be as powerful an anchor on your future as the inability to forgive others. I have had very few regrets in my life that have lingered. Some of them I finally realized were silly. When I was in high school, I really wanted to go to Duke. The campus was beautiful and in a beautiful state. They had a great basketball team. It was Ivy League without the Yankee and I qualified for a good scholarship. My mother insisted that, on my road trip to check out colleges, I go check out a small Baptist university in Macon, Georgia.

My dad and I took the father-son road trip alone. It was the first time I had ever traveled alone with my dad. I was not sure how it would go. But after years of not being able to spend a lot of time with him because of his work schedule, we had more than a week in the car together and he let me do most of the driving. He also insisted we take back roads so we could explore. We drove across Louisiana, Mississippi, and into Alabama on Interstate 20, then up to Montgomery. From there we ditched the interstate for U.S. 80. We got to go through Tuskegee, Alabama, and the Tuskegee National Forest. We listened to Paul Harvey. Then we made our way through rural Georgia, eventually getting to Macon.

Mercer was nice and the people were wonderful. Still, no one had ever heard of Mercer. I wanted to go to Duke. Instead of going directly there, to Durham, North Carolina, we drove up to Virginia to visit my oldest sister in Portsmouth. I had my fill of William and Mary, Washington and Lee, and even had a fleeting thought of the University of Virginia solely because of the Thomas Jefferson connection. We then made our way to Durham. There were wrecks along the way and traffic moved like molasses. We finally arrived in the late afternoon with sore butts and empty stomachs. We got lost finding the campus, and when we did find it, our tour guide was rude. I decided to go to Mercer.

For several years, I regretted it. I loved my time at Mercer, but it was no Duke. I knew I would never have had to explain to people where Duke was. During the summers, I would drive home to Louisiana and camp out at LSU in a fraternity house with one of my best friends. The college life at LSU was amazing, particularly with a drinking age of eighteen at the time, and I was pretty sure Duke would have been the same way. But not Mercer.

It finally dawned on me several years later that I was an idiot. Any experience I would have had at Duke was hypothetical. But all my experiences at Mercer were real. I made real friends, got a great education, and met my wife. I stayed for law school, got involved in politics, and worked for a law firm, and my career took off. Any regret Gunnar and Evelyn have because they did not do something is going to be premised on a hypothetical. What really should matter is what they make of what they actually did.

Holding on to regrets keeps us from moving forward and also keeps us from appreciating what we have. C. S. Lewis, in *The Screwtape Letters*, writes about this. Screwtape tells Wormwood to keep the human grounded in the past or the future, but never the present. The present is where God is and where life itself is. If a person lives in the past, they become convinced the present is worse than what they had. If they live in the future, they become convinced the present is worse than what will be. But if we live in the present, we appreciate what we have and see the past and future more realistically. We experience God in the present and receive his blessings in the present.

Regret, though, does not just come from the untried phantoms of past memories; it also comes from those things we did and should not have done. There are those things we do that we replay in our heads over and over, trying to undo wrongs or change outcomes. We linger on whether things could be different. Often we put aside these regrets and forget them. But a smell or a sound or the breeze on our face brings back these memories and guilt and wonder like ghosts haunting us.

Ginger Guthrie is one of my favorite people.

Growing up in Dubai, she was our librarian. A Vanderbilt grad who kept a home in Atlanta, Georgia, she was the first person to demand I read. She would settle for nothing less than constant reading and would not let me settle for the children's books that were age appropriate. I was reading the Hardy Boys, Nancy Drew, and then got into nonfiction and Greek mythologies. She made it competitive between several friends of mine and me: Who could read the most? Eventually Ginger moved on to other parts of the world, but she would always connect with us when we went through Atlanta, flying home to Baton Rouge.

After we moved home and I moved to Georgia, I would regularly drive to Atlanta to visit her. She would take me out for burgers and discuss life. As much as I was growing into a conservative, she was a liberal and insisted on pushing me on what I believed and stood for. She was always happy to know I believed something because I believed it, not just because someone told me to believe it. When Christy and I got married in 2000, Ginger had not yet met Christy, but my whole family was coming over and they all wanted to see her. We traded a few emails on directions to the wedding, with one final email from me with the time, date, and details of how to get there from her house. She never showed up.

A week and a half later, returning from our

honeymoon in Canada, I discovered that my last email to her had not gone through and I had a voice mail from her. She was stuck on the interstate trying to get to our wedding and had no idea where she was going. I tried to call her and could not get her. I emailed her and never heard back. For a while I worried she was mad at me, then for awhile longer I was mad at myself for not being more diligent. Only now, as I have composed these letters to my children, have I managed to track Ginger Guthrie down and reconnect. The loss of friends is perhaps one of the few regrets we never get over, particularly losing those we were so close to for so long.

What I have learned about regret is that we either control it or it controls us. What we do with regret is part of what makes us. We either learn lessons and move on or we let it weigh us down. Life is too short to hold on to things. It is too short not to forgive, because forgiving others means they can no longer control you. Life is too short to be buried by regrets. Learn the lessons from what you regret and move on. Appreciate what you have. Find the silver lining. Above all else, show others the grace and mercy they may not show you. There will be others who will never forgive. They will not forget. They will remind you and call you a hypocrite. But you must show them grace. It elevates you, and it is a reminder that we all do things we should not. You may never get them to stop reminding you of your past misdeeds, but you do not have to let them control your actions or force you to change course from what you know is right. And you never, ever have to worry, because it does not control you. Life is too short to be worried about what other people think.

# SIX

# THE ART OF SLEEPING WELL AT NIGHT

*Conscience Is Important*

Doing that which is right is rarely the easy thing. Often it may not make you popular. There's a reason cartoons will depict the devil and angel sitting on a character's opposite shoulders. We're all like that with voices screaming at us. One yells to do what is easy. The other yells to do what is right. Life is like that much of the time.

I have made things difficult for my family by doing what I think is right. We have had people show up at our home to threaten us. My children have been yelled at in the grocery store. At school, other kids have harassed them. But my kids know I did right and they understand. My goal for Gunnar and Evelyn is that when they grow up they are better than me. But that would be an impossibility if they never saw me modeling what is right. They need to see the unpleasant side of doing what is right and they need to know the benefit of a clear conscience. Above all else, they just need to know they should do what is right, not what is liked or easy.

I sometimes reflect back on a woman I met

once named Sheri. At the time I was preparing to leave my law practice, I was working on several indigent criminal law cases. I had the option of passing back these cases to the court system so the clients could have a new lawyer. Sheri, however, was problematic. Sheri had been in and out of jail. She was an addict, and had even prostituted herself in order to obtain drugs. She had stolen from family, friends, and others. Her life had hit rock bottom and she was finally in jail with no hope of getting out.

Going to the Bibb County Law Enforcement Center was never a pleasant experience. The air smelled. The people who were incarcerated there tended to be poor. The visitors' area reeked of cigarettes and alcohol. As a lawyer, I got to wade quickly through the crowd of visitors. A guard would lead me through the interior of the jail to a hallway with a series of rooms. The rooms had windows on the doors, but otherwise contained nothing except for cinder-block squares with a metal table and two metal chairs. Lawyers met their clients there.

I met Sheri shortly after Labor Day in 2005. She was in her thirties but looked much older. She had short, cropped reddish brown hair, moles up the left side of her neck, a large gap between her front teeth, and terrible breath. Sheri had been charged with drug possession and theft. She had stolen money from a family member to buy her drugs. The family member knew the only way to get Sheri the help she needed was for her to get arrested and locked up. But Sheri did not want to plead guilty. She insisted on fighting, even though she would privately admit her guilt. Still, even at rock bottom, Sheri had a level of pride that necessitated her not admitting to stealing from family. I finally persuaded Sheri to plead guilty. It took time and the intervention of her ex-husband. But she would do it. The alternative would be a trial in which she would most certainly be found guilty and then get a far worse prison sentence.

In October, we went before the judge and Sheri pled guilty. She would be kept in jail for six months. It would have been longer, but her relative went before the judge and explained he never would have had her charged with a crime but he knew Sheri needed treatment. She would not go away to prison, but would stay in a local facility where she could get treatment. It was a reasonably happy outcome to an unhappy situation.

I did not think I would see Sheri again, but one day in November as I was winding down my law practice, I got a collect call from the jail. Sheri wanted to see me. I had closed the file. She was no longer my client. I could not bill the time. Still, I went to see her. I remember that when she walked in, the first thing I noticed was the smell. She stank. And she was yellow.

Sheri was dying. During her years of hard living, she had damaged her liver, and it was giving up. She was not a candidate for a transplant. Sheri wanted out of jail. She wanted to die at home. It would have been really easy for me to walk away. I had notified the judges that I would be leaving my law practice. Most of my office supplies were packed up in boxes. But the right thing for me to do was to help her.

I reached out to the judge who had sentenced her and the assistant district attorney. They were both open to considering Sheri's case, but they would need a doctor's examination. Thanksgiving was coming, my new job was starting, and they could not get to anything until December. During my first week at my new job in Washington, I spent almost as much time on lining things up for Sheri as I did on the job. I even missed work to appear with Sheri in court. The doctors made clear what was obvious from looking at her: There was no point in leaving her in jail. Shortly before Christmas, in her ex-husband's house, Sheri died.

In retrospect, the role I played in helping Sheri be granted early release from her sentence seems like an easy decision. At the time, it was not. I hated practicing law, particularly criminal law. I hated going to jail. I disliked representing people who were guilty but argumentative. I liked drafting contracts and helping to facilitate transactions. Someone else would have been vastly more capable of helping Sheri. I did not get paid for all the work I did. But there was only me. To pass her off to someone else would have cost her time. And I knew she died in peace.

Working on indigent criminal defense cases was required in my county whether I wanted to or not, and it was a miserable experience. But it opened my eyes to a life I never really knew existed. I saw young men joining gangs because they had no family at home. I saw poverty and addiction. I saw illiteracy and joblessness. I saw crumbled families and drifting souls.

Sheri was my last client as a lawyer. As it happens, my first client had also been an indigent criminal defendant. Both cases taught me so much more than I expected. My first client is still one of my favorite stories as a lawyer. The man was charged with possession of crack cocaine. I met him the day before we had to go to court for the very first time. He was hostile and belligerent and convinced someone had framed him. But every time I asked him to describe the man, all he would do was snarl, "He looks like you, man." Clearly, the guy had issues. At the hearing the next day, I decided I need a psychological evaluation of my client. After all, he thought some man like me had framed him by planting crack cocaine under the driver's seat of his car. The assistant district attorney and I had agreed to a month's delay since I had just gotten the case. But when we got to the hearing in front of Judge Christian, the toughest judge in the circuit, I worked up the courage to ask if I could approach the bench.

"Your honor," I started, "this is my first indigent case. I don't know what procedure I need to go through, but my client needs to be psychologically evaluated."

"Why?" she asked, her glasses perched on the tip of her nose as she looked down at me.

"Well, he claims he was framed. He says some man put the crack under his driver's seat and called the police on him," I explained. "But every time I ask him to explain to me who he thinks framed him, he says the person looks like me. I am at a loss."

Judge Christian waved her hand, shooing me out of the way.

"Sir," she said, "stand up." My client stood.

"Do you mean *the* man?" she asked.

"Yeah!" he exclaimed. "The man set me up."

Judge Christian motioned for the man to sit back down and looked at me with a half-annoyed and half-bemused expression on her face. The assistant district attorney was trying not to laugh. "Mr. Erickson," she said, "your client isn't crazy. He's racist. He thinks the white man framed him."

I could feel my face turning a million shades of red.

"I'll discuss this with my client, your honor," I said. The assistant district attorney noted we had agreed to hold off for a month and the judge let us go.

The man pled guilty. A year later, I opened the newspaper one morning to read he had eventually gotten out of jail and was later killed in a shooting between rival gangs.

I never went to trial with any of my indigent clients. I would have been scared to death to do it. But I never had a client who was innocent. Many of them had terrible, mitigating factors. But all but my first were willing to plead guilty for what they had done. They might have had trouble acknowledging they had done wrong. Many of them denied it right up until they had to go to court. But guilty consciences force decisions and they finally decided to unburden themselves by admitting guilt rather than face harsher punishments by refusing to acknowledge what they had done.

On occasion, I could keep them out of jail if they had no prior record. Sometimes I could keep them from going off to prison so they could stay in the local jail. But a lot of times I saw already destroyed lives crumble away. The most surprising part of my job was how often the parents, if they were even around, had no clue what their children were involved in and with whom they were involved.

I know Gunnar and Evelyn sometimes get annoyed when Christy and I pry into their lives. One day, I hope they read all this and understand we did it because we love them. We punished them because we love them. We regulated their internet time and monitored who their friends were because we loved them. It is the right thing to do, and the older I get, the more I realize how few parents do it. We have until college, at least, to raise them right and prepare them for the world.

Knowing that Gunnar and Evelyn will often be forced to choose between the easy thing and the right thing reminds me of a story Steve Jobs told about his father. His dad, when building a fence, would make sure the part of the fence no one ever saw was just as nice to look at as the part everybody saw. Later in life, Jobs would design computers that distinguished themselves not just on the outside and through their interface, but even inside when taken apart.

Sometimes doing what is right is inconvenient. Sometimes it's hard to see the immediate benefit from doing so. Sometimes it is cumbersome or takes a lot of time. Sometimes it wears on you and disrupts friendships. When I started college, I took a Myers-Briggs test. I am an ISTJ, which I learned is what most judges are. My sense of justice is pretty off the charts. Occasionally, I have let it get the better of me.

As a freshman at Mercer University, I took a "freshman seminar program." Students could apply to take the "FSP" or go the regular route of taking electives. If you took FSP, you then got to substitute those credits for other classes. It wound up being an introduction to a world I had never experienced and would not soon forget. Country had definitely come to town.

My professor was as liberal as I was conservative. In her class, we explored trust, perspective, and bias, and even went on a camping trip as a class complete with trust falls and climbing walls. I had, since I was a kid, resented anyone telling me I had to do something that made no sense to me. Here we were being told to rappel down a several-stories-high wooden wall and I flat-out refused. Ever since I'd rolled off a mountain as a kid on a scouting trip in Dubai, heights and I did not get along. What were they going to do now, fail me for exerting independence? Honestly, I really wanted to rappel down that wall, but justice required standing up to the man or, in this case, the woman.

Having explored trust, perspective, and bias the first quarter, in the second quarter we would go further. The final class assignment required that we go to a gay bar and write about how it felt to be there. We were to examine our discomfort at the encounter.

Now, you might assume my outrage was over

going to a gay bar in particular, but I was a Southern Baptist going to a Southern Baptist university. I was not going to a bar of any kind, especially one where it felt more than a bit duplicitous to go. I was a Baptist! And I was supposed to go in order to describe what it felt. Egged on by a freshman roommate (he had once woken me up in the middle of the night to tell me, "I think we can be friends, but we both need to accept here and now that since you aren't Catholic, you're going to hell"), I refused to go and was then promptly informed that if I did not go I would be denied a passing grade.

Somewhere in me a political activist began to grow. This was an intolerable situation. I was not going to a bar, let alone a gay bar, as part of a college assignment at a Baptist university. I may have engaged in underage drinking, but I did it in the privacy of a dorm room, away from the eyes of other Baptists and legal authorities. So I did the only reasonable thing I could do. I sneaked into the closet of the President's Dining Room in the campus student center and stole a copy of the minutes of the board of trustees, which had the private contact information of each member of the board. As a member of the student judiciary, I had meetings in that room and knew someone had forgotten their copy of the minutes, which had then been placed on the top shelf of that closet for safekeeping. I had been nosy. Sue me.

I called every member of the board of trustees who had the letters *R, E,* and *V* in front their name. I introduced myself and explained my predicament. It was scandalous and I made sure to scandalize all of them. What would their congregations think? I even showed up at the church office of one of the trustees for added emphasis.

It was not more than seventy-two hours after I first started making phone calls that the provost of the university called and summoned me to his office. Dr. Horace Fleming was just about the nicest person you could ever meet and had a way of making you feel guilty for inconveniencing him. He had heard from the outraged trustees and he had a deal. I would take a C in the class, never set foot in the classroom again, and never, ever call any trustee ever again for any reason under the sun, so help me God. I had no intention of settling for a C, but he said my options were F or C and there would be no negotiation. I took the deal.

At the end of the quarter, the professor summoned me to her office. She stressed how very much she disagreed with me, but in her words "it took balls" to do what I did. She gave me a B. I never even thought of the matter again, but ten years later my wife was working as the assistant to the president of my alma mater. A lady who worked as the secretary for the FSP program had remembered all those years later the student who stood up for himself and would tell other students when they ran into problems about what I had done.

I did what I thought was right and would do it all over again. I hope Evelyn and Gunnar will stand up for what they think is right. But civility in the process is always necessary and often forgotten. I did not make a spectacle of myself and they do not need to, either. Quiet conviction is an underrated attribute.

Part of the FSP program that I did comply with was the insistence that all the students in the program involve themselves on campus. Some ran for student government. Others volunteered with Habitat for Humanity or worked in an office. I decided I would try out for the student judicial program. Not only did I get invited to join the program, but in just two years I would become the university's chief justice.

As if the third branch of student government weren't enough, I also served as the first branch of the student government as parliamentarian for three years. I was a bit of a dictator. I had no life on campus except the student government and judicial system. I poured myself into it. Every bit of student-drafted legislation suddenly took on the air of a congressional bill. I formatted everything, added line numbers, worked on white spacing, prepared official seals, picked appropriate fonts, and did my level best to give the objective advice an unelected parliamentarian was expected to give, but also pushed through improvements to the student code of conduct based on what I saw from the judicial system.

When I became chief justice, the dean of students let me change the system to work better and more efficiently. Naturally, I made it in my own image, which meant that appeals from lower courts would come to me. I could hear them myself or create a special court to hear them.

On July 27, 1996, Eric Rudolph planted a bomb in Atlanta's Centennial Olympic Park. The park was crowded with people. One person died and 111 others were injured. Rudolph went on the run and tensions in the Peach State remained high. Less than a month after the bombing, some geniuses in a fraternity decided to prank on a couple of their fraternity brothers. They filled two-liter bottles with aluminum foil that had been sprayed with oven cleaner, then screwed on the lids. Pressure built and the "bottle bombs" exploded. It just so happened that the fraternity brothers lived in an apartment complex with a lot of senior citizens. People flooded 911 with reports of explosions. Local police quickly tracked down the culprits and realized they were Mercer students. Instead of prosecuting them, they handed them over to the university to deal with, which passed them off to "my" judicial system.

Though they were not in the most popular or populous fraternity on campus, the individuals involved had lots of friends. Several of my own best friends on campus were members. I convened a lower student court and let them have at it. The accused fraternity members brought along their parents, a lawyer, and a donor to the university who had been a member. I did not want my judges to feel intimidated. Much to my chagrin, not only did they not feel intimidated, but I thought they failed to treat the situation with the seriousness it deserved. The local police had trusted the university to handle it and here was a student court slapping the students on the wrist.

In my arrogance as a twenty-year-old wielding way more power than a twenty-year-old probably ever should, I was hell-bent on making sure the students learned a lesson.

While I was sitting in the student courtroom watching the trial, the very same fraternity pledged my roommate. New members of a fraternity are called "pledges" and go through a period of testing their loyalty (*cough*—hazing—*cough*) before formally becoming a member of the fraternity. Here I was walking in my apartment in high dudgeon only to see my roommate of two years beaming that he'd been invited to pledge that fraternity. They had, however, assured him it was not related to the pending matter.

Blech.

As anyone who knows me well will attest, I am prone to doubling down when I think something is the right thing to do. Damn the torpedoes, I will go full speed ahead. They did not call me "Judge Dread" for nothing. Since the judges I had picked myself did not do what I thought was right, I decided I would hear the appeal all by myself. I had already made up my mind that they had no technical grounds for an appeal, but I would have to go through the motions. Then someone killed a squirrel.

The student prosecutor who handled the university's side of the case woke up the day of the appeal and found a murdered squirrel on her car. Having already been harassed by members of the fraternity, neither of us really doubted where the squirrel had come from. I was about to mount Johnny Cash's pale horse. The appeal was very straightforward. The student defender argued on technical grounds that the lower court had made mistakes, and also argued that the severity of the punishment was applied unfairly to the fraternity instead of to the individuals. The student prosecutor argued that the technical grounds were trivial, and, considering it was all members of one fraternity involved, there was every reason to prosecute the fraternity as being involved and failing to curb the behavior of its members—oh and by the way, anybody ever hear of the Olympic Park bombing?

I did what I thought I had to do.

Between dead squirrels and pledging my roommate, the fraternity had thrown me a curveball and by God I was going to throw them one even at the expense of friendships. I knew that the only way to make the situation right was to get an appeal to the dean of students. And I knew that the only way to get an appeal to the dean was for me to do the one thing I should not do. I upped the punishment by suspending the fraternity from campus and imposing hours upon hours of community service on the individuals involved.

The United States Supreme Court could take notes on how I formatted, phrased, and white-spaced that decision. I even debuted a fancy new signature underneath the ornate typography I selected. My arrogance had gotten the better of me. I saw a dear friend get his copy of the decision, open the envelope, and read. I could see his complexion change, his shoulders slump, and I realized I had made him cry. I felt pretty terrible. I got home and the phone calls started pouring in from outraged friends. The student defender called and tore me a new one. To this day I can remember him yelling, "You don't give someone the death penalty when they appeal a parking ticket!" I did not see my roommate that night. Or the next night. But when next I saw him, he was no longer a pledge in the fraternity.

Oddly enough, I remember closing myself up in my room and crying over that, of all things. My sense of righteousness had cost my roommate something that made him happy.

But I remained convinced I had done what was right. The people involved viewed what they had done as a prank. The local police had trusted the university to discipline the people involved, and I was willing to take the hit on friends and friendship to do what I was convinced was right—force the actual, real adults in the room to take action. And they did. The dean of students played good cop to my bad cop. He reduced their punishment to something vastly more reasonable than what I had given them, but vastly more severe than what they had originally gotten. They may have all hated me, but they got the punishment that fit what they did and were happy about it considering they would not be suspended from campus. There are friends of mine from college whom I have not spoken to since that day. Most of them got over it. They knew I did what I thought was right and were not going to hold it against me.

The week after I graduated, the student government promptly amended their constitution to prohibit a parliamentarian from ever serving as chief justice of the judiciary again. My elaborate but highly efficient judicial reorganization collapsed under its own weight. There may be no such thing as an indispensable person, but when you design a system making yourself the keystone, that system is going to collapse when you leave. It was a lesson I took to heart years later when I determined I wanted to quit a job where I was viewed as indispensable. I stayed two years longer than I had ever wanted just to make sure the whole thing would not go belly-up upon my departure.

In the last year I have often thought back on this formative experience in college. Last year was a year of testing and a year of doing what I thought was right.

I wrote a book in 2016 about Christianity and the struggles for Christians in an increasingly secular society. In February, on a book tour, I kept having a nagging thought. I needed to say what I honestly thought about the 2016 presidential race and how I could not bring myself to support Donald Trump. It was not just that I did not think he could win. As a conservative, I really wanted a Republican to win in 2016. But I thought Trump was a bad role model and not fit for the office. On a train back from New York City, where I had been on Fox News to talk about my book, I wrote a column explaining that I could never support Donald Trump for president. I did not think he could win, and even if he won, I thought he would be a disaster. My values transcend my political party and are premised on my faith. I thought too many people were wrapping their faith up in the various sinners running for president instead of relying on God. I wrote at one point that if God wanted Donald Trump to be president, God did not need my vote. Turns out he did not need my vote.

My friends were divided. Some of them are no longer friends. My radio station was inundated with complaints, to the extent that my boss was worried I might have ruined my career. President Trump took to Twitter to attack me, which made matters even worse. I could no longer fill in for national talk radio programs because the listeners to those shows would have revolted. The TV networks had no use for an anti-Trump Republican. Still, I thought I was doing the right thing.

Thankfully, not only did my ratings hold up, but they actually increased. I learned through this experience who my real friends were. But more important, I modeled for my children doing the right thing. Gunnar and Evelyn were champs. I worked hard to explain to them that though I may differ politically with people, we cannot treat people the way the soon-to-be president treated people and we could not behave the way some of his supporters were behaving toward us. I wanted them to understand that sometimes people put all their faith in people and people are sinners.

They are not perfect. But cults of personality are strong. People identify with people more than they identify with an abstract, invisible deity. They look on a person as their savior and model their behavior after that person.

If nothing else, the last year was a lesson in peer pressure. I realize what I'm about to say violates the current prevailing belief, but some peer pressure and bullying is okay. Evelyn would never have mastered riding a bike had her friends in the neighborhood not pressured her. Gunnar would have never gone exploring in the neighborhood creek had he not been pressured to do it. He was intimidated. Unfortunately, more often than not, peer pressure and bullying are used not to get you over a fear, but to make you conform or do things you should not do. The pressure to support President Trump was overwhelming. The number of people lining up to take my radio job shocked me. They were convinced I would lose it. One local host emailed my boss the day after the election to make sure our station knew he was available.

I was terrified. If my show got canceled, I would lose my health insurance. If I lost my health insurance, how could I pay for my wife's cancer treatment? What would we have to sacrifice to get the money? Would it be better if I had a "reluctant change of heart" and suddenly started supporting Trump? But I just could not do it. Luckily, a lot of Trump supporters made it easy. People who came out as reluctant supporters of Trump were treated just as savagely by Trump supporters anyway. There was no incentive to switch and even the thought of losing my radio show, losing my health insurance, and losing my wife could not persuade me that I should change my mind.

No one should ever do the right thing hoping for thanks or gain. Doing the right thing is the reward in itself. Our works may not get us into heaven, but I do believe we are going to be judged on our works one day. Those who do not believe in that last judgment might instead see it as karma. We should do the right thing, even though we sometimes fall short. The consequences may be steep. Sometimes the consequences are costly. And I know firsthand that there will often be people who, rather than patting you on the back, will be trying to drive knives into it. But—and this is a really big but— never underestimate being able to sleep. I worried for my family. I feared for my job. But I never doubted I was doing the right thing. Whether helping an indigent client or losing friends in college or losing friends in politics, I never once lost sleep. I never expected adulation or awards or accolades.

But I sleep well at night.

# SEVEN

# THE OTHER SIDE

## *Believe in God*

Evelyn and Gunnar are the center of my universe, but they are not the center of the universe. I keep pictures on my computer—pictures of family through the years posing for the camera and doing mundane activities. I will often scroll through those pictures at night, in my office, alone with no one looking, and try not to cry. I see my wife and me as a young couple. I see the few photographs of me as a child. Then I see my children and their cousins. I see how they look alike. I see how they are different. The faces, the eyes, and the smiles summon memories of days, perhaps some imagined or made more perfect than they were, but days of youth and innocence and joy. I want my children to stay innocent and young, but I know that the hard realities of the world beyond our home call to them, lure them, and tempt them away. I worry for them. I want them to know that they are loved so when they feel unloved or rejected elsewhere, they will know they can come home again.

Few things are as terrifying as the realization that the clock is ticking on how we raise our children. Will they be good? Will they love God? Will they fall away from the values we teach them? Will they be kind? There is a reason people do not get gray hair until they have kids. But then they have kids and the next thing you know, those kids are driving. Thankfully Evelyn and Gunnar are not there yet, but it is coming sooner than we realize, sooner than we want, and sometimes not soon enough.

Evelyn and Gunnar may be the subject of Christy's and my affection, but they need to know how insignificant they are in the universe to appreciate their significance. There are more than seven billion people on the blue orb of life that circles the giant ball of plasma that is the sun. There are nine planets, including Pluto (and damn the astronomers for saying otherwise), countless moons, asteroids, and objects at the outer edge of the solar system. Beyond is the Milky Way, with hundreds of billions more stars and countless other planets, comets, and space debris. But the Milky Way is just one of a seemingly infinite number of galaxies with a seemingly infinite number of stars in a vast expanse of space so large we cannot see it all. And it is all drifting steadily, farther apart.

I sometimes sit in the field behind our house with my telescope, looking up at the heavens. The Andromeda Galaxy lights up my telescope and the Orion Nebula's colors sink into my retina. When I was a kid, I would go camping with my dad in the deserts of the Middle East. We could see the Milky Way at night. It made me feel smaller than small. We are not even specks in the universe. The vastness of space is only paralleled by the vastness of our imagination to conjure up ideas about what is out there, but that sometimes makes us forget about what is already here. Some people look up at the night sky and see a random act of cosmic chance. I look up at the night sky and see the handiwork of our Creator.

God is real. I am convinced of it. No amount of scientific testing or explaining away of miracles can make me think otherwise. I do not expect that I can convince anyone who does not want to believe. It's like Graham's number. Ronald Graham "discovered" the number now named after him. I cannot write it out for you. Every atom of every particle of every object of every substance in the entire universe could be called up and used to write out Graham's number and it would still not be enough. The number is so large it cannot fit in the entire observable universe. But it is a real number. Add one to it and the number grows even larger. Multiply it by two and it grows larger still to a number now double the size of a number that cannot even be contained in the known universe, but real nonetheless. I would not expect that we could contain God in a universe of his own creation when math itself spills over the boundaries of the universe.

The orderly proposition of a mathematics that can explain the universe seems to bely a cosmic music that reveals order instead of chaotic randomness. As others have noted, when you work your brain back to the other side of the big bang and consider that there must have been something that gave rise to an explosion of unfathomable energy creating a universe, galaxies, a solar system with planets, and a planet with us on it—well, that something begins to look a lot like a god.

The God I believe in and raise Gunnar and Evelyn to believe in is the God of all creation. In the book of Jonah, the prophet boarded a ship of pagans to run away from the God I worship. When a great storm came up, the pagans cast lots and the lot fell to Jonah. All the pagans had gods. They had different gods. They questioned Jonah about his god. "Tell us on whose account this evil has come upon us. What is your occupation? And where do you come from? What is your country? And of what people are you? And he said to them, 'I am a Hebrew, and I fear the Lord, the God of heaven, who made the sea and the dry land'" (Jonah 1:7–9). His was not the god of wind or thunder. His was not the god of the sea or rivers or land. His was the God of it all. That is my God, too. His existence explains to me why we have something rather than nothing.

There are those who are persuaded that from nothing comes everything—multiverses and universes giving way to this universe all through random acts of science in the cosmos that we do not understand. Like Lucretius, the Roman philosopher, they believe in the swerve of atoms that randomly collide through infinite time, summoning life into existence. For them, there is nothing after death and nothing before life. Personally, I think we all have inside us a voice that tells us there is more than that. Some people do a very good job of suppressing that voice. I want Gunnar and Evelyn to hear the voice. I want them to ask why there is something instead of nothing. I want them to know God as much as he can be known. Like Graham's number, he can never fully be known, understood, or appreciated. But I look at the world and see great beauty. I look at the universe and see things hard to fathom. I look at people and see their need for interconnection and the need to know others. In all of that I see God.

The British clergyman William Paley illustrated this in 1802 with the idea of a pocket watch in a field. When you find the watch you do not presume that a random assortment of atoms collided together to make it. You see the hand of a watchmaker who attended to details with precision. That argument does not persuade everyone, but it persuades me. I see a complex universe woven with interrelation and vastness and see God in that. Belief in God does not require me to be anti-science. In fact, every day I get in a great aluminum and steel box, turn a key, and set off a series of small explosions of fuel and sparks that propel me this way and that. I am not trusting in God that those small explosions will not kill me, but in science and Henry Ford. I just presume that science cannot explain the full complexity of its creator any more than a watch can explain the full complexity of its maker. Both suggest a maker, but the maker lives outside both, putting his love and talents into them.

That Creator compels us to behave in certain ways. In the Hebrew Bible, the first verse says that God created the heavens and the earth. The verb choice for "created" is *bara*. It is a distinct verb choice for create. It only applies to the divine. When Noah built the ark, when the men built the Tower of Babel, and when Moses built the ark of the covenant, they did not *bara*. Only God can *bara*. God creates the heavens and earth. He creates us male and female in his image. He creates life. We do not have the power to do those things. This knowledge puts us in our place. We are created, not the Creator. We are handed creation and are to be good stewards of it. We are supposed to recycle and manage our resources. We are supposed to take care of our neighbors. We are supposed to love others and treat others with respect.

Why, then, do bad things happen? Well, sometimes they just do. That is not a satisfying answer, but God is not necessarily punishing us. He is not a sadist. There is no karmic imbalance. Life is just hard. God never promised it would be easy. Sin pollutes the world, rendering us fallible and feeble. God did not create evil, but he created a universe where evil was possible. Whether in the literal or metaphorical sense, the story of Noah is apt.

In the beginning, God created everything. He separated the heavens from the earth, then separated the waters from the dry land, then locked up the waters below the land. By the age of Noah, sin had become so corrupting that everything was undone in exactly the opposite order of what God had done. First the waters from the deep came up, then the waters and dry land merged as water covered the planet. All of creation was upended except a man on a boat with a family of sinners, left alive because that one man found favor with his God. The moment they got off the boat, sin went back into the world. It cripples our relationship with each other and with God.

God is very real. Sin is very real. We have obligations to our Creator and we are not ourselves the Creator. We cannot change what He created. But we are all going to fall short. I will disappoint my children. They will disappoint me.

We will get sick, get old, and we will all one day die. Sin crept into the world and we will work hard at being more like the divine, never fully succeeding, until one day we are free for eternity. Along the way, those of us of faith will see many with no faith do better than us, enjoy the world more, thrive and be thrilled. But we must understand that this world is the best they will have and this world is the worst we will have. All of us will get to eternity, but we will not all end up in the same place.

Recognizing all this requires that we forgive and show grace. It requires, in fact, that we be more forgiving and more graceful than those who do not believe these things. Others will hold grudges against us, never forgive, never forget, and declare us all hypocrites, but that does not mean we can reciprocate.

I do not expect to persuade everyone that there is a God. But I know what He has done in my life. I have felt His very real presence. I have seen opportunities presented that were unexpected. I have seen myself head off into a career I never even wanted or dreamed of, but now love. I have felt the warm embrace in times of distress when sitting in the mud crying that my wife would die. Scripture speaks of a peace that transcends all understanding. I have felt it. I want my children to feel it. But to feel it they must believe. In this world, understanding gives rise to belief. But with the things of the divine, it is belief that gives rise to understanding.

That understanding then shows us how far short we fall. That understanding shows me how my politics and faith sometimes do not align and that it is easier to align my faith to my politics, but proper and hard to align my politics with my faith. The former will allow me into a tribe of people who care greatly about the world. The latter will exile me from many who thought I was with them, but whose positions I cannot take because my faith will not allow it. Conforming to my faith is hard. Sometimes it is far harder than I expect. But I think it is necessary and makes me a better husband, father, and person in trying. It is that trying, not succeeding, that matters. The struggle is most important. When I feel burdened, or let down, or wonder why so much of it is hard and unfair, I think of Jesus on the cross. Martin Luther noted that there on the cross was the greatest sinner who ever lived. All the sins of all the believers before and after him piled on him at that one moment. So great was the sin that the sky went dark and the earth quaked. God turns His back on His own son because he cannot stand the sight of sin. The innocent man laid down his life for the guilty and through that act we are free. That freedom allows us to struggle with sin. We know we are going to keep failing even as we strive for perfection. We are all sinners. But our failures are covered over by our faith in Him who struggled and conquered death.

I want my children to know and believe these things because I believe them and believe that rejecting these things will separate us in eternity. But Gunnar and Evelyn need to go beyond rote belief. Belief is nothing without action on those beliefs. Christianity may be different between Catholics and Protestants on the role of faith and works in salvation, but both agree that works are part of faith. I believe that we are saved by faith alone, but we will have works to show we have that faith. This requires aid for others. It is our obligation.

That obligation is pretty straightforward. We are to help the widows, the orphans, the poor, and the refugees. It is an obligation we cannot pass off to others, but one we must take on ourselves. I remember when Evelyn, at eleven, was going through the process of joining the church. We had a long talk about what it means to join the church and submit to the discipline of the church. "Dad?" she asked. "Does this mean I have to go on mission trips?" I laughed. It does not. Perhaps she will want to go on a mission trip one day. But she does not have to. Frankly, I think a lot of churches take beach trips so their kids can work on tans and hammer a few nails so they feel good about themselves. I would rather my children donate their money than worry about their tan lines on a mission trip. I'd rather them pray for those in need and volunteer their time. Too many people say, "We pay taxes. The government takes care of it." But the government makes it all abstract. You do not truly know the needs of the poor until you have spent time with them. You do not truly know the needs of the community and those who help the poor until you invest your money with them.

We have three things we can give in life: our time, our talents, and our treasure. Sacrificing some of each is what scripture demands. That time may be time in prayer. Our talents may be in raising money or awareness. Our treasure cannot just be taxes. I am no opponent of a social safety net, but I am a strong opponent of justifying its existence as a way to get off the hook individually. Even though we have huge medical bills and debts, we still give as much as we can. We have provided food to those in need, money to organizations, and plane tickets to strangers we did not even know so they could go to sick or dying relatives. None of it was to brag. None of it was done publicly. All of it was a moral obligation. I write it here now not to brag, but so Gunnar and Evelyn might know that even in the struggles we have had with money and illness, we did not shrink from our obligation to others.

I am truly blessed. I never wanted to be on television and radio. I fell into it. Some people say it was luck, but I am not a lucky person. Other people say it is skill or talent, but I know myself better than them. I consider it all providential. Ultimately, when people try to get me to explain why I believe in a God and why I believe we have obligations to others, I can only tell them what I have seen in my life. My first vivid memory of anything related to faith was sitting in my grandmother's lap as she read me the story of Daniel in the lion's den and of Shadrach, Meshach, and Abednego in the furnace. There were many times I drifted away, but something always pulled me back. There was always the voice in the back of my head prodding me.

Events seemed to happen through God pulling the strings—not luck or accidents, but as if by design. My college roommate was engaged to a girl from Savannah, Georgia. The summer after our freshman year, he broke up with her and moved away. His former fiancée and her roommate stayed in school, but her roommate eventually transferred back to her hometown. Four years later, out of the blue, I got an email from the roommate. She had kept my email address after all these years. I never knew it, but she had a crush on me. She was taking a computer class and one of the guys in her class dared her to email me. She did. We were married about a year later.

All these things just sort of happened. I never

planned it or plotted it out. I spent a lot of time in prayer and God provided. He provided a wife, two children, and an amazing career. Again, I know me. I know my talents. I am not selling myself short. I have a face for radio and a voice for print, yet I am on television, radio, and in the newspaper. It was not me. If I died this minute and only had the energy to type four final words to Gunnar and Evelyn, it would be these: "Trust in the Lord."

Trust comes with an obligation: love. God is love. But people misunderstand what love is. Nowadays people think love is anything and if you do not love it as much as they love it, you are judging. That is just so world-centric and wrong. Please understand what love is. "Love is patient and kind; love does not envy or boast; it is not arrogant or rude. It does not insist on its own way; it is not irritable or resentful; it does not rejoice at wrongdoing, but rejoices with the truth. Love bears all things, believes all things, hopes all things, endures all things. Love never ends" (1 Corinthians 13:4–8).

Love is not passive. It is substantive. It rejoices with truth, but does not rejoice with wrongdoing. Love can be wrathful. Love requires discipline and punishment. If I did not love Evelyn and Gunnar I would never discipline them. But because I want them to be good, to be respectful, to be well behaved, and to love, I have to discipline them and admonish them. Yes, I have spanked them—rarely, and always followed by hugs—but I have spanked them. I see parents spoil their children thinking they are loving their children because they never discipline them, but they are really setting their children up to fail. Love has boundaries. Beyond those boundaries, love cannot exist. Love can spark a relationship, but love takes effort.

Sometimes people confuse loving and liking. There have been times where I have loved my children, but not liked them. I am sure they have felt the same toward me at times. Sometimes they misbehave. Sometimes they can be selfish. I always love them, though, and try to correct them because I love them. And I will love them forever. Yes, they may disappoint me. I may even disappoint them. But love can withstand disappointment. Love is a verb. Love is something we do. It is an action. God loved the world so He gave His son. His son loved the world so He gave His life sacrificially. I love my children so I work multiple jobs to send them to a good school and have their mother home with them. I hope they realize one day when they are sad that I could not make an event that I was working for them and their livelihood. That sometimes required I miss events I desperately wanted to be at. There are moments I will never have with them that Christy had.

Love has standards, too. Nowadays people think that if you don't love everything about someone, you are judging them. Nonsense. Love has to have standards and comport with our values. This idea that love is love is silliness. Where does love come from? Some would say it is a biological attraction. Perhaps, but long after that biological attraction fades away there is still love. I was about half the man I am today back when Christy and I got married, but she still loves me. Love is something more than biological attraction. Love is soul harmony—a by-product of two people becoming one in mind and body—and love is a feeling of connectedness. We get that connectedness from our Creator. He is love. He is wrathful and disciplines, but He is sacrificial and would lay down His life for us. We should never confuse infatuation with love. The former fades quickly and the latter will age well if properly nurtured.

Aging well in the twenty-first century is harder and harder, with social media and the record of our lives spread out in digital bits and bytes. The easiest impediment to relationship building today and finding love is flagged hypocrisy—that is, others making sure that those we wish to connect with know we are hypocrites. We have fallen short of some standard we hold. The reality is that we are all hypocrites, and if someone truly were not a hypocrite it would be because they had no standards. Standards are those things we set as right and proper. It does not mean we will get there. I am a hypocrite. I have done many things I regret, but I have also done many things others wished I regret that I do not.

Our integrity comes from recognizing we are hypocrites and flawed. But this does not mean we should give up having standards, morals, values, or principles. The world is very conformist, but that conformity drags us down to the lowest common denominator. We cannot have higher values than someone else or else we are accused of judging. We cannot tell anyone else they need to clean their act up or repent because we are judging. Everyone quotes "judge not lest you be judged" but they always forget that Jesus followed it up with "go and sin no more." The judging is not telling people they have fallen short of standards or lack character or otherwise sin. The judgment comes in deciding that the person cannot change or is not going to heaven. There are standards. Read any religious text and there are standards for living, behaving, and conforming to the religion away from the world. Noting that someone has deviated from those standards is not judging, but it is necessary in getting them to turn back. Judging is telling them they are going to hell. We can never do that, but we should never be afraid to note that others are not living as they should. Only in this day and age does that sound judgmental.

By setting standards and trying to live by those standards ourselves, we find our integrity. It is far better to be respected because of our integrity than to be liked. Everybody wants to be liked, but once we get over the need to be liked, perhaps then we can be respected. People may not agree with you on issues, standards, behaviors, or lifestyles, but we should be able to respect each other's differences and understand where those differences come from. Finding common ground in our differences is a life skill slowly being lost. As society grows more and more secular, it will be harder and harder to find common ground, but the quest is as important as actually finishing it.

My standards are set by my faith. I believe in a Creator who sent His son to die on a cross as substitution for my sins that I might have eternal life. All I have to do is put my faith in His son and I will be saved. But there comes a series of oughts from that. There are things I ought to do. There is a way I ought to live. And if the world comes into conflict with that, I should distance myself from the world. Eternity is at stake. How we live now reflects how we want to live on the other side of the grave.

I want Gunnar and Evelyn to know it is going to be harder for them than it was for me to live their faith in public. There will be so much pressure to conform. There will be so much pressure to give it up, decide it is not real, or otherwise water down their faith. I hope they take scripture to heart that if the world is applauding them, they are probably doing it wrong. That does not mean they should be jerks. It does mean they should follow God, not their friends. They should commit to His standards and surround themselves with like-minded believers. They should not want to be cool or liked, but they should want to be loved. I hope to model a community for them so that they may grow up and find a community of like-minded people with whom they can take refuge from the world. We may not be able to escape our world, but we all need a break from the howling winds of conformity.

# · EIGHT ·
# WE ALL HAVE
# A ROLE TO PLAY
## *Build Strong Communities*

I put off writing this chapter until the end. One day I hope and presume Gunnar and Evelyn will sit down and read this. I want them to have a sense of who I am and answers to both the how and why Christy and I raised them as we did. One of Evelyn's teachers once congratulated me. They had never had a parent whom they did not feel comfortable googling in class to show the kids how the internet works—never had one until me. My kids need to know the things I am not proud of as well as those I am proud of. This now must be written and it is painful to write. I have alluded to it and danced around it and now must confront it.

There is a story in the New Testament. In the fifth chapter of Mark, which most Bible-believing Christians accept as Peter's account written by the disciple John Mark, Jesus performs an exorcism:

They came to the other side of the sea, to the country of the Gerasenes. And when Jesus had stepped out of the boat, immediately there met him out of the tombs a man with an unclean spirit. He lived among the tombs. And no one could bind him anymore, not even with a chain, for he had often been bound with shackles and chains, but he wrenched the chains apart, and he broke the shackles in pieces. No one had the strength to subdue him. Night and day among the tombs and on the mountains he was always crying out and cutting himself with stones. And when he saw Jesus from afar, he ran and fell down before him. And crying out with a loud voice, he said, "What have you to do with me, Jesus, Son of the Most High God? I adjure you by God, do not torment me." For he was saying to him, "Come out of the man, you unclean spirit!" And Jesus asked him, "What is your name?" He replied, "My name is Legion, for we are many." And he begged him earnestly not to send them out of the country. Now a great herd of pigs was feeding there on the hillside, and they begged him, saying, "Send us to the pigs; let us enter them." So he gave them permission. And the unclean spirits came out and entered the pigs; and the herd, numbering about two thousand, rushed down the steep bank into the sea and drowned in the sea. —Mark 5:1–13 (ESV)

"My name is Legion, for we are many." Cast into the nearly two thousand pigs, the herd charged down a bank into the sea and drowned. Had Peter continued with this story he would have noted that the demons, upon leaving the dead pigs, all got Twitter accounts. I am increasingly convinced social media is of the devil. Many people, many good people, have anonymous accounts on social media and let loose a torrent of vile and unseemly ideas. They wish ill on others. They say things they would never say if their name were connected to it. Sometimes they even do and say things they do not believe, but love to provoke a reaction. Trolls come out from under a bridge and harass, intimidate, yell, and otherwise make life on the internet a terrible place.

I have behaved like that, regrettably. Unlike most trolls, I did it under my own name.

In 2009, Justice David Souter retired from the United States Supreme Court. A friend, on a group email, made a statement we all thought was awful, but awfully funny at the same time. The friend, smartly, decided he should not put it on social media. But I did. My tweet referred to the retiring justice as "a goat f\*\*king child molester." Even now, all these years later, I cringe just writing these words.

With the group email, it was just my friends and me. With Twitter it was tens of thousands of other people, many of them people who considered me worth following because they valued, though not necessarily agreed with, my opinion. I did my level best that day to destroy all my credibility.

Piled on from all sides, my response was to double down and refuse to apologize. I had said something people did not like and they could deal with it. But the kernel of guilt had already been planted. In less than a week, but longer than it should have taken, I apologized. The impetus for my apology was a friend in trouble who needed to be defended, but I could not defend her without first apologizing for my own actions and using myself as the example of being wrong.

All this time later, the incident still comes up. Some people seem to relish bringing it up. Almost a decade later, some would define me still by that tweet. No amount of apology can ever be enough. When I publicly rebuke someone for their bad behavior, others throw this old tweet in my face. It is used by those who do not like me to undermine my credibility. No interview with the press ever passes without it coming up. No profile in any magazine lets it pass. It will, no doubt, be in my obituary as that which I am most famous for. "The evil that men do lives after them; the good is oft interred with their bones."

It was a terrible thing that I wrote—a shameful thing. As someone who tries to live out my faith, it undercut that ability. The first question in the Westminster Catechism asks, "What is the chief and highest end of man?" The answer: "Man's chief and highest end is to glorify God, and fully to enjoy him forever." I had failed at my chief task. Not only had I not glorified my Creator, but I had hindered my ability to attract others to Him and reflect Him in my life.

In a way, though, I am glad it happened. I was utterly clueless in how my work affected my family and friends.

Even after apologizing publicly, I found my wife days later crying in our kitchen. Having to apologize to her was harder than apologizing publicly. She was hurt. People who would never come up to me to question me or berate me were doing it to her. She got the awkward questions. She got the hard questions. Everyone avoided me and she bore the brunt of it. Her family had to deal with it. Some of her relatives read about it in the local paper. It makes me nauseous just to think about it.

Never once had I ever considered my family would be impacted by what I said, wrote, or did. Never once did I think I would have to worry about them. The whole experience was eye-opening. It forced me to realize that there were others who did look up to me. Moreover, I had a family who really did support me and could be disappointed in me. People who I presumed were passive players in my life were actually active participants.

A year later, when CNN hired me, all the people who hated me swirled into the fray demanding the hiring be undone because of that one tweet.

It was a self-inflicted scarlet letter. I remember that as pressure mounted to have my contract canceled I was in a Toyota dealership, about to buy my first new car ever. I had to call my boss at CNN and ask if I could sign the contract for the car. Luckily, the network showed me grace others wished they would not show me.

Gunnar and Evelyn need to know that others will always seek to define me by the bad things I have done and it will happen to them too. My generation was blessed to grow up before social media and the internet. Our worst temptations could be constrained because we had no access to anonymous online outlets. My children will not be so lucky. They will not be able to escape from anything they do. The internet is forever and there will always be those who refuse to show grace or forgiveness unless they conform.

I have no doubt in my mind that if I abandoned my principles and convictions, I would be embraced. I see it happen all the time. The people who conform their values to the herd are forgiven or ignored. Those who do not are always forced to relive the bad things they did. My children, you, and I must resist the temptation to abandon our principles because we have fallen short of them. The world roots for us to do that. Legion has Twitter accounts cheering you on to fail and embrace the failure.

The mob mentality of social media is one of

its worst aspects. Any person or business may have the mob summoned against it. If the social media mob disagrees with a business owner's views, it will harass the business and try to ruin its reputation until the business owner conforms. Disagree with a person's politics, religion, views, votes, or even clothing choices and watch the mob pick up digital pitchforks to demand apology and conformity.

Just as dangerous, political and polite disagreements can be magnified, amplified, and weaponized. Say something provocative or disagreeable and watch as others attempt to harm you with it. There are, to this day, things I have done and said that others think I should apologize for. As much as I have learned that I must apologize when I have done something wrong, the equally valuable corollary has been to hunker down and weather the storm of social media scorn and mob demands for conformity when I believe I am right and Legion thinks I am wrong.

Social media, a mob mentality, and demands for conformity make it more and more important that we know who we are. We need to know how we define ourselves and how we honestly should be identified. We cannot be merely the accumulation of our tweets or Facebook posts. We must be, and we are, more than that. Each of us is created in the image of God. We are sons and daughters of others who came before us. Our parents have aspirations for us and we have aspirations for our children. We have neighbors, family, and friends.

In my time running two websites and interacting with people who made their names on the internet, I have learned something important. The people whose lives are defined by their internet personae are typically the most maladjusted people I know. It is not necessarily that they are socially awkward, but that they are oftentimes bitter and frequently cannot accept that they are to blame for their own problems. Everyone else is to blame. The people who seem the most normal online are most often those grounded in the real world, who have families and church attendance and civic participation.

Gunnar and Evelyn are going to be challenged, as will all children. They will see people who are "YouTube famous" and be tempted to give it a go themselves. The internet is an alluring place. Legion will try to absorb them, define them, and conform them. But I want my children to live in the real world. I want them to have unique, strong identities as individuals created in the image of their Creator, loved by their parents, and put on this planet to glorify God and leave it better than they found it. The world is a physical, dirty, often unseemly and untidy place. The internet amplifies much of it, but often ignores the good. I want my children to find their meaning and existence offline in a world of physical relationship, not long-distance digital relationships.

Community is that which is around us and that of which we are a part. We may belong to an online community, but that online community cannot nourish us, does not provide ties that fully bind us, and is more abstract than the real community around us. As people become more and more fixated by the online, our communities are breaking down around us. Fewer people know their neighbors. People who used to sit on their front porches or the front stoop of their building are now in front of glowing screens absorbing them. They no longer see the things that go on around them.

When Gunnar was five years old we took a trip. I had given him my iPad loaded with movies. Instead of watching the movies, he delightedly watched the map. That blue dot of where we were, showing where we were headed and showing what we were passing. "There's a river coming up!" he yelled excitedly. "We're going over the river," he said.

"Look out your window!" Christy yelled back to him. But no, he was fixated on the glowing screen. He never once looked up to see the Chattahoochee River pass under us, with boats and kayaks and fishermen. He was instead on satellite mode on the iPad, watching it on the screen. The real world passed him by without him ever seeing it. He is not alone in that regard. More and more people are like that. But it should not be so.

Next door to you is a person called a neighbor. That person has real needs, hopes, desires, aspirations, problems, and joys. That person may very well be willing to look after your pet or your home when you go away. Your Facebook friend cannot do that. Being willing to know our neighbors and be neighborly is a lost art. The world has gotten so tribal, we now identify with causes, not communities. The cause becomes our community. But the cause as community gets monotonous and swiftly one can find one's self kicked out of the community for deviating from the orthodoxy of the cause. When the cause becomes the community, the community is small, homogeneous, and perhaps too comfortable. Real community should be comfortable, but should always have the potential to discomfort us. That discomfort makes us care.

As we recede into the digital bubbles of homogeneity that pass for community but are really just the Potemkin villages of a comfortable mind, it becomes easier to turn a blind eye to the homeless man who lives under the bridge in your town or the child being abused or the family barely making ends meet. They are not part of "the cause," so they are not part of your concern. But you must make it your concern to care for those in your local area. You simply must. If the internet went dark tomorrow, the people on your street would still exist.

Within your local community, and as a respite from the world at large, build a smaller community. Break bread with people. As a general rule of thumb, no person is a truly terrible person unless it is impossible to share a meal with them. I have encountered such people. I have encountered the rabid conservative whose bile and tunnel vision make it impossible to enjoy the food on the table. I have encountered the bitter feminist who views every statement as a sleight and every joke as out of bounds. I have encountered the Christian whose zeal for the Lord in casual conversation makes my zeal for the plate in front of me disappear faster than my kids when the dishes need washing. I have also encountered the atheist academic so incapable of talking of anything besides his nonbelief that I had to excuse myself from the table. But those are the rare exceptions.

I have found, in building community, that it is possible to enjoy a meal with most anyone. It is all the more refreshing to break bread with those whose politics do not align with my own, because the conversations are so much more interesting. They turn to life and love and youth and adventure. With one of my dear friends whose politics are completely opposite mine, we talk of our okra gardens and gumbo. With another, it is shotguns. Learning to cook and inviting people around the dinner table builds community that lasts. Building that community with people who disagree on politics can be adventurous, but richly rewarding because of the effort it takes to find common ground.

One community that also must not be ignored is your church community. On more than one occasion, Christy and I have thrown open our doors to members of our Sunday school class and others in church. Instead of cooking an elaborate meal, we just invite people over to throw whatever they bring on the grill, let the kids play, enjoy a drink, and visit. This is the part of community building that is more important than any other and the one Evelyn and Gunnar should prioritize, as should we all.

The Western world is becoming more and more secular. It is leaving behind many of the values that people of faith cherish. We must build up community with others who disagree, but we must tend to the community of like-minded believers. There are those who would say we should let our children go out into the world and make up their own minds, find their own ways, and develop their own beliefs. But that suggests our beliefs do not matter or are relative. I believe in eternity and judgment. That must affect how I raise my children. That must affect how my children go out into the world.

I want my children to engage the culture around them, to be a part of their local community, and to be an example for others to model. But that requires they see examples modeled in their own lives. That requires Christy and me to surround ourselves with like-minded people. The day will come when Gunnar and Evelyn get to an age where everything their parents do will be invalid, bad, or wrong. But they will look to our friends—the parents of their friends—and they will either see our lives mirrored or they will see something that is different from our lives. If they see the same values, they will be more likely to understand the seriousness and importance of those values.

I know some people may disagree with this, but I do not truly believe anyone ever really lets their children find their own way in the world. That would be irresponsible. We cannot guarantee the success of our children, but we all have aspirations for them. As someone who tries to take his faith seriously, my chief aspiration for my children is that they glorify God and enjoy Him forever. Pop culture, television shows of the day, the internet, the kids at school, the evening news, and the world in general are less and less aligned with that aspiration. That obliges me to make more of an effort at it.

I know there are people who think we should just build a high wall around our homes, cut the cables, and never leave. I have friends who have withdrawn their children from school, turned off the television and internet, and begun homeschooling in earnest. It is like a new Amish community. But even the Amish recognize their children might venture into the real world. I think we must prepare our children, but prepare our children truthfully. If I tell my children that chocolate is of the devil and disgusting, but one day they are tempted and take a bite, like Adam and Eve suddenly aware of their nakedness, my children will be suddenly aware their father is a liar. If they then question my truthfulness on chocolate, they are going to start questioning everything. I want my children to reflect my values and the morals of the church, but I do not want to lie them into it. I do not want to sequester them from the world so thoroughly that they long to find out what is out there. I do not want them to be lost to the big world, but to introduce them to it so that they may swim in it, but not get pulled away by the secular currents and tide of the day.

World-weariness has gotten me. Of course the Germans have a word to sum it up: *Weltschmerz*. The Germans have words to sum up everything. But it does not quite mean what I wish it to mean. What I mean is that I find myself more and more tired of the daily fighting in politics and culture. From bathrooms to legislative fights, everyone is supposed to have a side, join a tribe, and be in each other's face. We pick apart 140 characters on Twitter and decide we can know a person's intent, personality, life existence, and level of humanity. We all need a retreat from world-weariness, and community is the best solution short of an isolated beach house.

It is trendy these days to have "safe spaces," but in reality there should be just one safe space—your home. And in your home, you should invite your friends and neighbors to meet on neutral ground to share in life free of the cultural and political battles everyone is increasingly forced to take sides in. No one should ever expect a safe space outside their home, but in their home they should break bread with all comers who are willing to be respectful and kind to one another, even though they may disagree on various issues.

Community should overcome tribe. Tribalism has invaded our lives and pulled us toward the primitive and guttural, where nuance has no place. You must like Taylor Swift or Adele. You must like the president or not. You must say good things about him or nothing good about him. Tribalism shuts out honest brokers, those who would think for themselves, and those who see a multifaceted world. We stereotype others and place them in tribes instead of treating them individually. We grow suspicious of those who refuse to conform to our tribe or who have friends in other tribes. We should all resist the tribe. Our faith, family, and country must come before tribal divisions that pit us against them, encourage victimhood, and silence the other.

That then gives us some level of purpose in life. I have noted our chief purpose is to glorify God, but what in our day-to-day lives does that? First and foremost, I think it is just treating others respectfully as creatures made in the image of God. There are those who think we have to do something bold with our lives—Christians who think we have to join the next mission trip or we are not fully part of the tribe, Republicans who think we have to cheer on the party leader or we are not fully part of the tribe, Democrats who do the same, and law firm partners who think we must devote ourselves to our firm ahead of our family. Everyone knows someone who thinks the chief end of man is to be dedicated to some cause that person thinks is extraordinary or a testament to loyalty.

The reality is that God is there in the dirty diaper that the mother changes because she gave up a career or took time off work to see to her children. God is there in the stack of bills on the husband's desk as he tries to make ends meet. God is there in the textbook of the student studying for an exam on a subject he privately knows he will never use again. God is in all those places. He is in the ordinary, the monotonous, and even the dull. Our purpose is to be the best we can be and shine even in those dull, ordinary acts. Our cheerful disposition in approaching the ordinary shines a light for others to see.

Our purpose, then, is to lure others to the light in all that we do. It is to provide a welcoming home, the smell of comfort food, the friendly smile, and the table around which the weltschmerz fades.

Be a good neighbor. Be the shelter from the storms of life. You will find that others serve that role for you. Be the voice that others can turn to and learn from even if they disagree. And be better than me at it. I fail. I sometimes let out my inner jerk when I should not. Other times, I see people intentionally or unintentionally completely misunderstand what I say, trying to drive outrage where there really was none intended. The internet amplifies that, makes it easier to do, and makes the misunderstanding take on the character of truth. That does not absolve us of our obligations to be a good neighbor. It does make us mindful that we should not live on the internet. It should also encourage us to surround ourselves with people who support us, hold us accountable, and sustain us.

When my career started growing and I started engaging more in politics, I found more people wanted my attention, support, time, or voice for their cause. Two friends decided it would be worthwhile to start a small group that could run interference for me, pass along information to me, and shield me; we could all help each other. That group holds me accountable for my actions, pushes me to do what is right, and shields me when needed. I know one of my great weaknesses is that I hate to tell people no. So the group makes it harder for people to even get access to me. The group of friends, my producer, and the team of people around me take stress from my life because I know I do not have as much free rein as I might once have had. I have others who support me, who will tell me honestly that I have screwed up, and who I can trust to be candid with me. Most of us met initially online. But we worked to build real, lasting relationships offline.

My worldview is centered around Genesis 1:1. "In the beginning, God created the heavens and the earth." God "bara," or God divinely created in a way that we cannot. Moses's writing was as countercultural then as it is now. It is extremely countercultural to say such a thing now. You'll be accused of believing the world is six thousand years old and be laughed out of the room. At the time Moses wrote these words, he wrote directly against an Egyptian cosmogony, which believed the gods, plural, had created everything and that most things were themselves gods.

Here comes Moses, raised a prince of Egypt, who informs everyone their entire cosmogony is wrong. Everyone else believed there were multiple gods who brought the universe into existence. This one guy tells them there is only one God and none of them are His chosen people. But he makes other bold assertions. The sun and moon were not gods, but just objects in the sky. So too are the stars. They are not to be worshipped and they have no divine meaning. God made them. It was both countercultural and bold.

Then God made the plants and animals, and lastly, he made us. He made us male and female, and united both in a complementary relationship where the skills of the wife and the skills of the husband aid each other in common purpose. That purpose is to be married, give new life, and steward the world. That cosmogony is completely countercultural now. It was when Moses wrote it as well. But there is more.

We get something from nothing. The Creation account provides us an answer to what came before the big bang. In fact, "let there be light" provides us the big bang. A Catholic priest, Georges Lemaître, came up with that theory and other scientists at first rejected it, believing Lemaître was just trying to justify the Genesis account. People of faith, when asked what comes before the big bang, would say God, and when asked what comes before that, would say God in all eternity. People who are not believers often have no answer for what came first and some even think the question illegitimate. But God is there and He gives us purpose.

We are creatures, not creators. We can create, but the things we create are less than ourselves or no more than ourselves in the case of procreation. We are not gods. It is no coincidence that those who question the existence of God most strongly are more likely to believe in the rise of machines and artificial intelligence that can enslave us. Some of the very scientists who reject the idea of God even now study to see if we are in a computer simulation like the Matrix. If we are, would not the creator of the program take on the appearance of God? And, in fact, even barring that, would not the force that gave rise to the existence of the big bang and all creation take on the characteristics of God?

Scripture tells us God created us in His image. That image gives us a sense of relationship between us and the planet and between us and other people. We are to be stewards of plants and animals and to have dominion over them. We are not to value our animals more than we do other people. We are, in fact, supposed to have relationships with other people. We are to love and be loved, to be good neighbors, to get married, and to multiply if we can. We have an obligation to marry and try to have children. Not everyone can, but everyone should try. We also get a deeper meaning of relationship. We encounter a God who walks with his people until sin disrupts that relationship. Even then, he dwells with his people in a tent—he tabernacles with them. Ours is a tent-dwelling God.

In the Bible, King David tells the prophet Nathan that David will build a temple for God and God says not to. God says, "I have not lived in a house since the day I brought up the people of Israel from Egypt to this day, but I have been moving about in a tent for my dwelling" (2 Samuel 7:6). Our God wants to be with us so much and to have a relationship with us so deeply that the Creator of the entire universe was perfectly willing to camp in a tent ferried through the desert. He wanted a relationship so badly with us that He sent His son to die on a cross in our place that we may be restored to Him. That paints a picture for us of the relationship he wants us to have with others and with him. We should be willing to tent with those who need companionship in uncomfortable, gritty places and times. We should be sacrificial in our love for others.

The need for relationships and community is why it pains me to have to acknowledge what a jerk I have been and can still be on social media. It is why I increasingly view social media as a bad thing. We are to build community and be relational with others. That requires both civility and a respect for differences. It requires we recognize that our lives have purpose. We may not know individually what our unique purpose is, but we cannot doubt that we have one. We should not give up on finding that purpose, but sometimes that requires simply trusting God. My life is a testament to the fact that God leads and we should follow. There have been so many times I did not know where I was headed, but found the destination greater than I could have planned for myself. There have been just as many times where I was fully convinced I knew where I was headed and wound up being surprised.

We should be the person who buys the losing lottery ticket and gets overwhelmed with excitement at not winning, knowing that if God did not intend us to win the $100 million jackpot, God must have something truly even more amazing in store for us.

# • NINE •
# BREAK BREAD LITERALLY
## *Cooking Brings People Together*

I really want a cooking show. I would call it "The Kitchen Cabinet" and I would invite on celebrities, politicians, and others to not talk about politics. Instead, we would cook a meal and have a conversation about life, our upbringing, and explore how our worldviews formed and shape us. The show would be dedicated to building community. I have always believed that we should be able to find common ground with others even if we cannot agree on politics.

For me, that common ground is food. I would love to talk chocolate with Nancy Pelosi, Las Vegas buffets with Harry Reid, and Tex-Mex with Ted Cruz. Bobby Jindal and I could talk Cajun food and Indian food while Jerry Brown and I discuss almonds and avocados from California. There would be beer on tap, a fryer, and bread. The whole gluten-free craze would be out the window. Jesus ate bread with gluten. You can too unless you are really allergic.

When I was five years old, I was a picky eater. My mother had enough. My diet consisted of raw spaghetti, cold hot dogs, and hamburgers heavy on the ketchup. (I am "blessed" with children even pickier than I was.) So fed up with me was my mother that she bought me a stool and a pot and told me to cook for myself. My first grown-up dish, as a five-year-old, was Flemish carrots from a cookbook my aunt LaVerne and uncle George had sent us from Belgium. I did not even eat it, but it was grown-up and exotic. So I ate cold hot dogs.

When I got older I kept cooking. In Dubai, some WWF wrestlers visited and came to our home several nights for dinner when I was in the third grade. One night, I cooked them cornflake chicken and gingerbread men for dessert. Tony Garea, Jimmy "Superfly" Snuka, Tito Santa, "Rowdy" Roddy Piper, and Playboy Buddy Rose sat around our dining room table and chowed down.

In high school, if my parents had to leave town, I would be home alone. Instead of raiding my dad's liquor cabinet or throwing keggers, I would open all the windows, bake pie, make homemade pizza, and invite my friends over. In college, I would make large pots of gumbo and jambalaya. Even now, Christy and I love for people to come over and eat. We never do anything formal and often we serve the same dish, but we simply love bringing people together for laughter, conversation, and community.

If I should die before my children wake, here

are the recipes I make (did not intend for that to rhyme) for them and for our family, with a few others thrown in for good measure. I hope they grow to love cooking like I do. So many of my most cherished memories involve being in the kitchen with relatives who have passed on. I remember my great aunt Daisy making her gumbo. My grandmother, an otherwise terrible cook, would get up every Sunday morning and make the best pancakes. Mealtime is memory-making time.

Oh, and one note for good measure—cookbooks lie. They tell you to "sauté the onion until brown, approximately 10 minutes." That is crap. It takes 25 minutes at least to properly brown an onion. Allegedly, cookbooks tell you this so you don't think the recipe takes too long and skip it. Cooking requires patience.

# APPETIZERS

## SPINACH-ARTICHOKE DIP

This is one of the snacks we make when guests come over. It is nice and warm and delicious. Truth be told, I was never a fan of this dip growing up. But Christy and I moved to a small church after her mastectomy. Carol Jordan, our pastor David's wife, made it, and I fell in love with it. This is not Carol's recipe, but it is darn tasty and easy to make for a crowd. Occasionally, I make it just for Christy and me. We wind up throwing half of it away, but sometimes you just need a warm snack.

    2 cups grated Parmesan cheese
    1 (10-ounce) box frozen chopped spinach,
       thawed
    1 (14-ounce) can artichoke hearts, drained
       and chopped
    1 cup cream cheese
    ⅔ cup sour cream
    ⅓ cup mayonnaise
    1 tablespoon fresh lemon juice
    2 teaspoons minced garlic

1. Preheat the oven to 375°F.
2. In a small casserole dish, mix together the Parmesan cheese, spinach, and artichoke hearts. Combine the remaining ingredients and mix them into the spinach

mixture. Bake for 20 to 30 minutes, or until hot and bubbly. Serve with crackers or toasted bread.

## PIMENTO CHEESE

Every family in the South has a pimento cheese recipe. I seem to recall my mother making one that was cooked. My wife's family keeps it simple. In fact, they don't even measure out stuff, but I did so for this exercise.

I have a sordid history with pimento cheese. Moving back to Louisiana from Dubai, my mother reintroduced it into our diets. In the South, you can buy pimento cheese at the grocery store. I would have pimento cheese toast almost every night. One time, after a trip to Virginia to see my oldest sister, I came home and made six pieces of pimento cheese toast. I savored every bite of that bubbly browned nirvana. I spent the next twenty-four hours revisiting every bite as I knelt before the porcelain throne. I never touched it again until Christy and I got married.

1 (16-ounce) block medium-sharp cheddar cheese, finely shredded
1 small jar diced pimentos, drained and chopped into small bits if necessary
1 cup Light Miracle Whip
2 teaspoons salt

Place the finely shredded cheese in a large bowl. Add the pimentos. Add the Miracle Whip and stir. Sprinkle the salt over the cheese and then stir it in. Cover and refrigerate. Add additional Miracle Whip as needed. Serve with Frito scoops.

## SALSA

Make salsa in a large blender or food processor. You may have to prepare it in batches. But this is a wonderful recipe. If it is too spicy for you, use just one jalapeño. Christy and I make this for friends and everyone thinks we must slave over it. Not only do we make it a day ahead so everyone can continue to think that, but it also tastes way better after a day in the fridge, once the flavors have blended.

1 (28-ounce) can whole tomatoes with juice
2 (10-ounce) cans Ro-Tel diced tomatoes
    and green chilies with juice
¼ cup chopped onion
1 clove garlic, minced
2 or 3 jalapeños, cut in half, seeded, and
    cut in quarters
1 tablespoon chopped fresh cilantro
½ teaspoon sugar
¼ teaspoon salt
¼ teaspoon ground cumin
Juice of ½ a lime

Combine all the ingredients in a blender or food processor and process to your desired level of chunkiness. I go smooth. Refrigerate the salsa for at least an hour. If you can't figure out the vehicle by which to get this into your mouth, perhaps you need to skip the recipe.

# BREADS

## ASPHODEL PLANTATION BREAD

Where I grew up in rural Louisiana, there was a plantation home called Asphodel, which had a restaurant. People would drive for hours to eat there and everyone wanted the bread recipe, which was a bit unusual. It was not your typical bread, but it was tasty. I make this for friends when I need a relatively quick bread. It rises pretty fast and takes about an hour and a half to make.

6 cups Pioneer or Bisquick baking mix
¼ cup sugar
½ teaspoon salt
2 cups warm milk
2 (¼-ounce) envelopes active dry yeast
4 large eggs
¼ teaspoon cream of tartar

1. Sift the baking mix, sugar, and salt into a large bowl.

2. In a smaller bowl, combine the milk, yeast, and a pinch of sugar. Set aside until it gets foamy.
3. In a third, even smaller bowl, whisk together the eggs and cream of tartar. Then whisk this into the milk mixture.
4. Add the combined milk mixture to the dry ingredients and stir to combine. It will be more of a batter than a dough.
5. Cover and let rise until doubled in size, then punch down with a wooden spoon.
6. Grease two 8-inch bread pans and pour the batter evenly between the two pans. Raise the pans up above the counter by about 6 inches and drop to force air bubbles to the surface.
7. Let the batter double in size again. Meanwhile, preheat the oven to 350°F.
8. Bake for 20 to 25 minutes, or until browned.

### HOMEMADE FRENCH BREAD

Christy's and my parents are deeply perturbed that we are members of a Presbyterian church instead of a Southern Baptist church. They wanted our kids to be dunked and, frankly, Christy wants the kids dunked. Instead, Evelyn went through the Presbyterian communicants class to join our church in fifth grade. After making her public profession of faith and joining the church, we had a dinner on the grounds. I made the bread. This was the recipe. It makes two loaves and is delicious. There was not a piece left. If you make my gumbo recipe (see page 190), make this bread to go with it. You will not be disappointed. And your house will smell wonderful.

2¼ cups warm water (see Note)
2 tablespoons sugar
2 tablespoons active dry yeast
1 tablespoon salt
5½ to 6 cups all-purpose flour, divided, plus more for dusting (I use King Arthur.)
2 tablespoons vegetable or olive oil
1 large egg beaten with 2 tablespoons water

1. Pour the warm water into a small bowl. Add the sugar and stir to dissolve. Sprinkle the yeast over the water. Sprinkle the salt over the yeast.
2. Fit your stand mixer with the dough hook and add 5 cups of the all-purpose flour to the mixer bowl. Make a well in the center and add the oil. Add the yeast mixture to the flour (be sure to scrape the sides of the bowl to get all the sugar and salt out). Turn the mixer on low speed and mix until a dough forms. The dough should be sticky and cling to the sides.

Add another ½ cup of flour and knead on low till mostly incorporated, then move to medium speed. If the dough is still stuck completely to the sides, add another tablespoon or two of flour. Knead in the mixer for a minute. The dough will be moderately sticky.

3. Oil a large bowl, then oil your hands. Scrape the dough out of the mixing bowl, shape it into a ball with your hands, and place it in the oiled bowl. Cover it for 15 minutes.

4. Sprinkle the tabletop with flour. Punch down the risen dough, place it on the table in the flour, and flatten it. Fold a third of the dough onto itself, then fold the other side, like folding a letter. Pat it down, turn it ninety degrees, and fold it in thirds again. Repeat the whole thing again. Make sure the bowl is well lubricated and add the dough back and cover. Let the dough rest for 30 minutes.

5. Repeat the process of folding the dough on a floured table, then return it to the bowl.

6. Preheat the oven to 375°F. Place an oven-safe pan on the bottom rack of the oven as it preheats.

7. Once the oven is preheated, divide the dough into two equal portions. Cover

one half with a damp cloth and shape the other into a rectangle. With hands or a rolling pin, flatten and stretch it to 18 to 20 inches long. The dough will be elastic; if it pulls back too much, just let it rest for 5 minutes. Should it become elastic again, let it rest for another 5 minutes.

8. Once the dough is rolled, make sure the long edges are relatively straight. Fold it over onto itself to ensure that the edges are straight. Then roll it up like a log. Importantly, pinch down the length of the seams and all the edges to ensure a tight seal. If you do not do this, you will have flat bread.

9. Place the dough on a parchment-lined baking sheet, cover with the damp towel, and repeat the process with the second dough ball.

10. Once both are formed, score the tops of both with three slits, then lightly brush with the egg wash.

11. Measure 1 cup of water, open the oven, pour the water into the preheated pan, then place the baking sheet with the bread on the rack above for 30 minutes. Rotate the baking sheet halfway through for even browning if necessary. The steam will help make a crunchy crust.

12. The bread will sound hollow when

thumped at the end. You can store it in an airtight container for up to a week, but it will not last that long. I like to take a stick of salted butter, let it get soft, stir into it ½ teaspoon of garlic salt and ½ teaspoon of dried parsley flakes, then spread that on the bread slices. Yum.

Note: I heat up about 2½ cups of water in the microwave for 1 minute, then measure out 2¼ cups. I find it gets to the right temperature without getting so hot as to kill the yeast.

## HONEY-BUTTERMILK BREAD

This is a great bread recipe to make for friends when they're under the weather or just need some home cooking. It is also the base for the Croque Monsieur (page 193) that I love to make and eat. I modified this recipe from one I found on the internet. The first time I made it, it fell flat. Turns out you really need no more than an 8 x 4-inch baking pan. If you use a 9 x 5-inch pan, it won't rise as much.

1 (¼-ounce) envelope active dry yeast
1 teaspoon sugar
Pinch of ground ginger (helps activate the
   yeast)
¼ cup warm water
2 cups warm buttermilk

⅓ cup honey

1 teaspoon salt

¾ teaspoon baking soda

6 cups white bread flour

4 tablespoons (½ stick) unsalted butter, melted and slightly cooled, plus more for brushing

1. Using the dough hook on an electric mixer, mix the yeast, sugar, ginger, and water. Set it aside and let it get foamy for 5 minutes.

2. Mix the buttermilk, honey, salt, and baking soda into the yeast mixture. Add 3 cups of the flour and mix for about 5 minutes, until smooth. Mix in the butter.

3. Now, with the mixer on low speed, add the remaining 3 cups of flour, one cup at a time, thoroughly incorporating before adding the next cup.

4. When the dough pulls away from the sides of the bowl, turn the mixer speed up to medium and let it knead the dough for 5 minutes.

5. Place the dough in a greased bowl, drizzle oil over the top, and roll the dough to fully cover it in oil. Cover and let rise for 1½ hours.

6. Punch down the dough, divide it in half, and place each half in a greased 8 x 4-inch

bread pan. Cover and let the dough rise for 45 minutes. Meanwhile, preheat the oven to 400°F.

7. Bake for 30 minutes. Brush the loaves with melted butter when they come out of the oven.

# BREAKFAST

Breakfast at the Ericksons' is truly something to behold. When my family comes for Thanksgiving, I make a giant batch of sausage and egg bake and French toast casserole. Unfortunately for me, though, everyone always demands my cinnamon rolls. The cinnamon rolls are a labor of love. They are time consuming to make, but worth it for special occasions.

### SAUSAGE AND EGG BAKE

I never had this till I got married. Christy's family has it for every morning gathering. For any holiday, this is getting made. The great thing about it is you can make it the night before, then just put it in the oven the next morning. It cooks well with the French toast casserole. I always serve the two together so people get something savory along with something sweet.

6 slices white bread, crusts removed
Softened salted butter, for buttering

173

1 pound bulk sausage
½ onion, finely chopped (optional)
5 large eggs
2 cups half-and-half
1 teaspoon salt
1 teaspoon dry mustard
½ cup shredded cheddar cheese

1. Grease a 9 x 13-inch casserole dish.
2. Butter the tops of the slices of bread. Place them, butter-side up, in the casserole dish.
3. Brown the sausage (and onion, if using). Drain.
4. Whisk the eggs, half-and-half, salt, and mustard together.
5. Sprinkle the sausage over the bread. Sprinkle the cheese over the sausage. Pour the egg mixture over everything. Cover and refrigerate overnight.
6. Preheat the oven to 350°F.
7. Bake for 40 to 50 minutes.

Note: As a variation, I sometimes use a 2-inch-round cutter and cut the bread into circles, place them in greased muffin pans, then make them as muffins (they'll bake in half the time). Then you can keep them in a bag in the fridge and put individual ones in the microwave. As a bonus, the edges are all crispy.

# FRENCH TOAST CASSEROLE

I love, love, love this recipe. It is a family hit. One time I made it in a Pyrex imposter and the moment I took it out of the oven it exploded, with shards of glass flying all over the place. That was an experience. I should change the name to "exploding French toast" or something. In any event, if this does not get made when my family comes to visit, there is rioting.

1 (1-pound) loaf challah or French bread, cut into 1-inch cubes
8 large eggs
2 cups half-and-half
1½ cups 2 percent or whole milk
2 teaspoons vanilla extract
¼ teaspoon ground cinnamon
¾ cup (1½ sticks) unsalted butter
1½ cups brown sugar
3 tablespoons light corn syrup

1. Butter a 9 x 13-inch baking dish. Evenly spread in the bread cubes. In a large bowl, beat together the eggs, half-and-half, milk, vanilla, and cinnamon. Pour over the bread, cover, and refrigerate overnight.
2. In a small saucepan, combine the butter, brown sugar, and corn syrup. Cover with a lid, but do not cook it.

3. The next morning, preheat the oven to 350°F.
4. Heat the butter, brown sugar, and corn syrup until bubbling. Pour over the bread and egg mixture. Bake for 40 minutes, or until brown.

## MONKEY BREAD

This is another recipe from Christy's family that I had never even heard of until we started dating. Now whenever my parents visit, my dad expects this. When Evelyn was a toddler, we would find her sneaking into the kitchen trying to eat the leftovers.

18 frozen yeast rolls
1 (3.5-ounce) box cook-and-serve butterscotch pudding mix
½ cup (1 stick) unsalted butter, melted
¾ cup brown sugar
1 teaspoon ground cinnamon
½ cup chopped pecans

1. Grease a Bundt pan liberally. Cut the yeast rolls into quarters. (Allowing them to thaw for 15 to 20 minutes to soften will make it easier.) Spread them evenly around the bottom of the Bundt pan. Sprinkle the pudding mix over the yeast rolls. Mix together the butter, brown sugar, cinnamon, and pecans. Pour evenly over the rolls. Set

in the oven to rise overnight.

2. The next morning, turn the oven on to 350°F. Bake, through the preheating stage, for 30 minutes, or until golden brown.

Note: Yeast rolls (such as Rich's) typically come in a bag of 36. Occasionally they will be in a bag of 18, which is the size needed. The brown sugar may be upped to a total of 1 cup if desired.

## QUICHE

I dated a girl once who worked in a restaurant that had quiche on the menu. One time a lady came in for lunch and ordered the quickie meal because she was in a hurry. Luckily the quiche was served up fast. I laugh about it every time I make a quiche. This is easy and good, and you can make it yourself. Yes, real men do eat it.

1 ready-made pie crust, chilled
½ to 1 cup chopped vegetables (no more than three types)
½ cup chopped meat (no more than two types)
¾ to 1 cup shredded cheese (no more than two types)
3 large eggs
1¼ cups half-and-half or whole milk
½ teaspoon salt
¼ teaspoon freshly ground black pepper

1. Preheat the oven to 375°F.
2. Put the pie crust in a pie pan if it is not already in one. Line the pie crust with parchment paper and add pie weights or dried beans. Bake for 20 minutes, or until set. When the pie crust is done, reduce the oven temperature to 350°F.
3. Meanwhile, sauté your vegetables and cook your meat if necessary.
4. Mix the vegetables, meat, and cheese together in a bowl and transfer to the pie crust.
5. Whisk together the eggs, half-and-half, salt, and pepper, then pour the mixture on top. Bake until the filling is set, 40 to 50 minutes. Let cool for at least 30 minutes before slicing.

Note: My personal preference is either finely chopped onion and spinach mixed with Colby Jack or Havarti cheese and bacon with ham or sausage.

## CINNAMON ROLLS

Let us be honest for a minute: This is the reason my kids love me. I confess it all started with some mild passive-aggressive competition with my wife. She was making cinnamon rolls for us, but I was used to the big, flaky style of cinnamon rolls that you get in bakeries. I saw a recipe in a Food Network magazine but did not quite like it. So I modified it to my tastes. Now my family demands I make these, friends demand I make them, and random strangers who follow me on social media come up to me when I am out to ask for the recipe. They take time, but I map out the time for you here. Make them at least once and you will be hooked. These are full of fat and do not skimp. But you must try them. Just remember that if your yeast is not foamy after 5 minutes, you probably killed it. Err on the side of too cool rather than too warm. If you get the milk over 110°F, you have murdered the yeast. Lastly, you can use this basic sweet dough for doughnuts, too. Just roll the dough out to about ¼ inch, cut them out, let them rise for 1 hour, then fry them. But the dough is meant for this recipe.

## INGREDIENTS FOR
## THE BASIC SWEET DOUGH

½ cup water
½ cup whole milk
1 (¼-ounce) envelope active dry yeast
¼ cup plus 1 teaspoon granulated sugar
4 tablespoons (½ stick) unsalted butter,
    melted and slightly cooled, plus more
    for brushing
1 large egg yolk
1½ teaspoons vanilla extract

2¾ cups all-purpose flour, plus more for
  dusting
¾ teaspoon salt

1. Begin at 8:00 p.m. the night before.
2. Warm the water and milk in a saucepan over low heat until a thermometer registers 100° to 110°F. Remove from the heat and sprinkle the yeast on top, then sprinkle with 1 teaspoon of the sugar; set aside, undisturbed, until foamy, about 5 minutes.
3. Whisk the melted butter, egg yolk, and vanilla into the yeast mixture until combined. In a mixer, whisk the flour, the remaining ¼ cup sugar, and the salt. Slowly add the yeast mixture and mix until a sticky dough forms. Increase the speed on the mixer and knead till the dough is elastic, about 3 minutes.
4. Coat a large bowl thoroughly with nonstick cooking spray (or softened butter). Shape the dough into a ball and add it to the bowl, turning to coat lightly with the spray. Cover with plastic wrap and let rise at room temperature until the dough is doubled in size, about 1 hour 15 minutes.
5. Turn the dough out of the bowl and knead briefly to release excess air; re-form into

a ball and return to the bowl. Lightly butter a large piece of plastic wrap and lay it directly on the surface of the dough. Cover the bowl tightly with plastic wrap and refrigerate for at least 4 hours or overnight.

## INGREDIENTS FOR THE CINNAMON ROLLS

⅓ cup granulated sugar
2 tablespoons ground cinnamon
1 batch basic sweet dough (see above)
¾ cup (1½ sticks) unsalted butter, softened

For the glaze
1¼ cups confectioner's sugar, sifted
4 tablespoons (½ stick) unsalted butter, melted
3 tablespoons whole milk
½ teaspoon vanilla extract
Pinch of salt

1. Make the rolls: Butter a 9 x 13-inch baking dish. To be clear—this recipe is not healthy in any way, shape, or form except for the soul. You've gotten this far. Use freaking butter to grease the dish.
2. Whisk the sugar and cinnamon in a bowl. On a floured surface, roll out the dough into a 10 x 18-inch rectangle. Spread the

butter over the dough, leaving a 1-inch border on one of the long sides. Top with the cinnamon-sugar over the butter. Brush the clean border with water. Tightly roll the dough into an 18-inch log, rolling toward the clean border; pinch the seam to seal.

3. Measure out every 1½ inches and cut a small score line on the top of the roll to mark your place. Slip a long, taut piece of thread under the roll, lift the ends of the thread, and cross them over the roll, pulling tightly to cut off a piece. Repeat every 1½ inches, to make 12 rolls. Place the rolls in the greased dish.

4. Cover the rolls loosely with plastic wrap and let rise in a warm place until doubled in size, about 1 hour 10 minutes.

5. Preheat the oven to 350°F.

6. Uncover the rolls and bake until browned, 25 to 30 minutes. Let cool for 10 minutes in the pan.

7. Make the glaze: Whisk the sifted confectioners' sugar, melted butter, milk, vanilla, and salt in a bowl until smooth. Drizzle over the warm rolls.

8. Devour.

9. One community-building note here: If you know someone is going to need good comfort food, you can bake these, then

freeze them, tightly covered, for up to two weeks. Just let them thaw completely, warm them in a 250°F oven, then add the glaze.

# SOUPS

## CHICKEN CURRY

When I was growing up in Dubai, Anna was our housekeeper, or "house girl." All the American families had a house girl. Anna and her husband lived in a very small building behind our house. Her husband drove an ice cream truck and they were saving money to be able to bring their children from India to Dubai. My parents had been hesitant about having a housekeeper, but Anna won them over, and her family became a part of our family. At night, when my parents were out of town, Anna would stay up in my room, which was also the TV room, and we would watch the Friday night Indian feature film together, beamed from Bollywood. It was an experience. Whenever we would take a trip, we would come home and find a warm pot of curry on the stove. I never got Anna's recipe, but I worked backward until I found one that was in every way like hers. The first time I tasted this, I literally cried. I was home.

3 tablespoons vegetable oil
4 whole cloves

1 cinnamon stick (optional)
2 bay leaves
1 small yellow onion, chopped
1 tablespoon grated fresh ginger
2 cloves garlic, minced
2 tablespoons plus 2 teaspoons mild curry powder (see Note)
1 tablespoon hot curry powder (see Note)
1 tablespoon sugar
2 teaspoons salt
1 teaspoon ground cinnamon
1 teaspoon Hungarian paprika
4 boneless, skinless chicken breasts, cut into bite-size pieces
1 cup coconut milk
1 cup plain yogurt
1 tablespoon tomato paste
½ teaspoon cayenne pepper
Juice of ½ lemon
Cooked rice, for serving

1. Heat the vegetable oil in a 5-quart Dutch oven over medium heat. Add the cloves, optional cinnamon stick, and bay leaves. Let sizzle for 2 minutes. Discard the cloves and cinnamon stick, if used. Leave the bay leaves in the pot.
2. Sauté the onion until lightly browned. Stir in the ginger and lightly brown for 2 to 3 additional minutes. Stir in the garlic and

brown for an additional minute. Stir in the curry powders, sugar, salt, cinnamon, and paprika. Continue stirring for 2 minutes. Add the chicken pieces. Cook and stir, scraping the bottom of the pot, and let all sides of the chicken whiten. Add the coconut milk. Stir in the yogurt, then the tomato paste, then the cayenne pepper. Bring to a boil, reduce the heat, and simmer for 30 minutes.

3. Remove the bay leaves and stir in the lemon juice. Simmer for 5 more minutes. Serve with the rice.

Note: I use Sharwood's curry powder. If you cannot find both hot and mild curry powder, just use 3 tablespoons of any available curry powder, but only 2 tablespoons if it is labeled a hot curry powder.

## CHICKEN AND DUMPLINGS

Christy loves chicken and dumplings. Perhaps it is a Southern thing, but this is comfort food for her. A friend in our Sunday school class makes chicken and dumplings, and every time Christy is unwell, she wants it, but she is too shy to ask for it. I finally decided I had to figure out how to make it. I got a bunch of recipes together and, as with all Southern food, there were a million different variations on how to make it. I put bits and pieces together and can now satisfy my wife's craving for comfort food.

1 (3¾-pound) chicken
½ teaspoon garlic powder
¼ teaspoon dried thyme
2½ teaspoons salt, divided
½ teaspoon freshly ground black pepper,
  divided
1 teaspoon chicken bouillon granules
3 cups self-rising flour
½ teaspoon poultry seasoning
⅓ cup vegetable shortening
2 teaspoons bacon drippings or
2 teaspoons cold butter plus ¼ teaspoon
  salt
1 cup cold milk

1. Place the chicken in a large pot and cover it with cold water. Add the garlic powder, thyme, 1¼ teaspoons of the salt, and ¼ teaspoon of the pepper, and bring to a boil over medium heat. Cover, reduce the heat to low, and simmer for 2 hours. Remove the chicken and reserve the broth.
2. Cool the chicken for 30 minutes, then shred the meat, tossing the bones and skin. Skim the fat from the stock, then return the meat to the pot. Add the bouillon granules and the remaining 1¼ teaspoons salt and ¼ teaspoon pepper.
3. Combine the flour and poultry seasoning

in a bowl. Cut in the shortening and bacon drippings with a pastry blender until crumbly. Stir in the milk. Place in the freezer for 10 minutes to chill. Turn the dough out onto a lightly floured surface, minimizing contact with your hands so it does not warm too much. Roll the dough to ⅛-inch thickness, then use a pizza cutter to cut out 1-inch pieces. You will want to use them all.

4. Drop the dumplings, a few at a time, into the broth, stirring gently. They will swell. Leave for a minute before each addition. When all are added, cover and simmer, stirring often, for 25 minutes.

## CHICKEN NOODLE SOUP

This is what Christy and I make each other when we are sick. One shortcut variation you can use is to roast chicken breasts rubbed in olive oil, salt, and pepper. Use 2 quarts of chicken stock and shred the meat into the stock. That is way easier, but less tasty. An old hen simmered for five hours yields a brilliantly flavorful stock and lots of meat.

1 hen or two small fryer chickens
1 cup finely chopped celery
1 cup chopped carrots
2 cups wide egg noodles

1 tablespoon kosher salt
1 teaspoon freshly ground black pepper

1. Put the chicken in a large stockpot or Dutch oven and cover with water so that the water just covers the bird. Turn the heat on high and keep close watch on it. Just before it comes to a boil, turn the heat to low and leave on the stove for 3 hours if using fryers and up to 5 if using a large hen. The hen takes longer, but yields more and tastier meat.
2. Remove the bird and save the stock. Strain the stock to remove any bits of skin or bone and return it to the pot. Shred the meat and return it to the pot. Add the celery and carrots and bring to a boil. Add the pasta, salt, and pepper. When the pasta is soft, the soup is done.

## BAKED POTATO SOUP

This is Christy's recipe. She went to Amelia Island, Florida, once with her friend Katie and had baked potato soup at a restaurant. She was convinced she could do better. And she did. This is so unhealthy and it is so, so good. When it gets cold outside, we both crave this. With a side of corn bread, it is perfect.

8 to 10 red potatoes
2 pounds bacon

1 cup (2 sticks) unsalted butter
1 large sweet onion, finely chopped
⅔ cup all-purpose flour
8 cups whole milk, plus more as needed
1 (16-ounce) block medium-sharp cheddar
  cheese, shredded
8 ounces sour cream
1 tablespoon salt
½ teaspoon freshly ground black pepper
4 green onions, chopped

1. Bring a pot of salted water to a boil. Add the whole, unpeeled red potatoes and boil till soft.
2. While the potatoes are boiling, cook the bacon in the microwave or a skillet until crisp. Crumble after cooking.
3. Place the potatoes in a bowl of ice water to cool to room temperature, then cut into bite-size cubes. Leave on the skin.
4. In a 7-quart stockpot or Dutch oven, melt the butter over medium heat. Add the onion and cook till lightly browned. Whisk in the flour until smooth and stir for 2 minutes to remove the raw flour taste. Gradually stir in the milk, whisking constantly until thickened. Stir in the potatoes. Bring to a boil, stirring frequently. Reduce the heat and simmer for 10 minutes. Mix in most of the bacon

and cheese (reserving some of each for garnish), the sour cream, salt, and pepper. Continue cooking, stirring frequently, until the cheese is melted. Add extra milk to thin as desired.

5. Serve, topped with green onions and garnished with extra bacon and shredded cheese.

## ERICK ERICKSON'S GUMBO

This is the dish my wife's family insists I make at Christmas and Thanksgiving. In fact, on Thanksgiving night every year I make a big pot and use the turkey leftovers instead of chicken. Several times a year, I make a huge pot and we invite our friends over. I rarely make seafood gumbo, because Christy does not like shellfish, but when I can, I will.

There are various names for various gumbos. Some people call it gumbo ya-ya. Gumbo mélange is gumbo with meat, poultry, and seafood. Fresh French bread is usually the bread of choice to dip into the roux. As for the roux, do not be intimidated. A while back I filmed myself making the roux in real time and put it on Vimeo and at The Resurgent. Just search for "Real Time Cooking" and you will find a link to The Resurgent's video. But the basics are this: Keep your stove on medium heat, use the large burner, and whisk constantly for 30 minutes. You should not burn it. Some people will tell you that your roux is too light. Some will tell you your roux is too dark. The reality is that there are as many gumbo recipes as there are Cajuns. This is mine and it is special to me and my family. This is my community dish that brings people of all walks of life together.

1 cup plus 2 tablespoons vegetable oil, divided
1½ cups all-purpose flour
1 pound andouille sausage, cut into ¼-inch rounds (Don't use spicy andouille—find Savoie's.)
1 medium yellow onion, finely chopped
3 stalks celery, finely chopped
1 large bell pepper, seeded and finely chopped
1 tablespoon Tony Chachere's Cajun seasoning
1 tablespoon salt
1½ teaspoons freshly ground black pepper
1 teaspoon dried thyme
½ teaspoon cayenne pepper
2 cloves garlic, minced
4 to 6 boneless, skinless chicken breasts, cut into bite-size pieces
4 bay leaves
8 cups chicken stock
2 cups chopped frozen okra
Cooked rice, for serving

1. Heat 1 cup of the oil in a large Dutch oven over medium heat. Sprinkle in the flour. Stir constantly with a whisk for 30 minutes.
2. When the roux is the color of a used copper penny, add the sausage and stir with a spoon. The sausage will begin to bow in shape. When the sausage begins rendering its fat, add the vegetables and seasonings, stirring constantly. After the vegetables have softened, make a well in the center of the pot, add the garlic to the well, then stir for 1 minute. Add the chicken. Stir and cook till the chicken is mostly all white. Add the bay leaves.
3. Add the chicken stock and bring to a boil. Once boiling, reduce the heat to low and simmer, stirring occasionally, for 1 hour.
4. After an hour, heat the remaining 2 tablespoons of oil in a skillet. Add the okra. Cook until the edges begin to brown and the seeds pop. Add to the gumbo and bring to a boil. Remove the bay leaves. Pour the gumbo on top of the rice and serve. (But note that gumbo is tastier if cooled overnight in the fridge and reheated the next day.)

Note: If you wish to add seafood to the gumbo, in addition to or instead of the chicken and sausage, add it after the okra, allowing the gumbo to boil for at least 5 minutes to cook the seafood. Shrimp, crab, oysters, and crawfish are traditional additions. An additional 32 ounces of chicken stock can be added for more gumbo without watering down the roux.

# MEATS

## CROQUE MONSIEUR

When I was a kid, my family went to Paris. Or rather, we had a layover in Paris and, miraculously, nobody was on strike. We did not spend a great deal of time in the city. Mostly we just stayed at the airport. My mom knew French and I was starving. She taught me how to say I wanted hot chocolate. Then she told me, in lieu of a hamburger, I should get a croque monsieur, which was what the French called a ham sandwich. It came and I was unsure of what to make of this thing in front of me. It was certainly a sandwich of some kind. But it was covered in cheese, the bread was thick, and it was exotic to me. But I was starving, so I took a bite. It was a life-changing event. Reading *Bon Appétit* magazine a few years ago, I stumbled on a recipe and doctored it to my tastes. Now I cannot live without this recipe.

4 tablespoons (½ stick) unsalted butter
¼ cup all-purpose flour

1½ cups whole milk
2 tablespoons sweet honey mustard
Kosher salt
8 (½-inch-thick) slices Honey-Buttermilk
Bread (page 171) or country white bread
6 ounces ham, shaved
1½ cups grated Gruyère cheese (or
Fontina)

1. Make the béchamel by melting the butter in a medium saucepan over medium heat until foamy. Add the flour and whisk until the mixture is pale and foamy, about 3 minutes. Gradually add the milk, whisking until the mixture is smooth. Keep whisking until the sauce is thick, about 4 minutes. Remove from the heat and whisk in the honey mustard; season with salt.
2. Preheat the oven to 425°F.
3. Spread the bread slices with the béchamel, dividing it evenly and extending it all the way to the edges. Place 4 slices of bread, béchamel side up, on a parchment-lined baking sheet; top with the ham and half of the cheese. Top with the remaining slices of bread, béchamel side up, then top with the remaining cheese. Bake until the cheese is brown and bubbling, 10 to 15 minutes.

Note: The sandwiches can be made (but not baked) one day ahead.

## WHITE BARBECUE CHICKEN

If we have people coming to the house and need a good, easy meal, this is what I make. Christy handles the sides and I man the grill. This is a hit every time we make it.

3 cups mayonnaise
⅔ cup apple cider vinegar
½ cup plus 2 tablespoons fresh lemon juice
¼ cup Lea & Perrins Chicken Marinade (green label)
¼ cup sugar
¼ cup cracked black pepper
4 to 10 boneless, skinless, chicken breasts, cut diagonally into strips

1. Whisk together the mayonnaise, vinegar, lemon juice, Lea & Perrins, sugar, and pepper. Add the chicken strips to a gallon-size Ziplock bag. Pour half of the sauce over the chicken and marinate in the refrigerator for 4 to 8 hours.
2. Use a quarter to a half of the remaining sauce for basting the chicken while it is on the grill (brushing every few minutes and flipping the chicken over halfway through).
3. Heat the remainder of the sauce over

medium-low heat, stirring occasionally, until it is steaming and becomes light brown on top. Use the heated sauce as either a dipping sauce or to pour over the chicken when serving.

## SPICY DR PEPPER SHREDDED PORK

Let me talk for a moment about Ree Drummond, aka the Pioneer Woman. My wife fell in love with her website years ago, and Ree has been a real prayer warrior for Christy during Christy's battle with cancer. We have never met Ree in person, but her recipes are regular staples in our home. Christy has a life goal of going to Oklahoma and helping Ree's husband brand cattle or some such. I am personally afraid she and Ree would run off to get tattoos together. Nonetheless, my children love her cookbooks because they are beautiful and easy to follow, and my wife and I love her recipes. Christy got this one and doctored it to our tastes, and it has become a regular in our home. Christy always makes this one in a giant clay pot. It also has Dr Pepper in it, which is God's favorite drink.

1 large onion
1 (5- to 7-pound) pork shoulder (also known as Boston butt)
Salt
Freshly ground black pepper

1 (11-ounce) can chipotle peppers in
  adobo sauce
2 (12-ounce) cans Dr Pepper
3 tablespoons brown sugar

1. Preheat the oven to 300°F.
2. Cut the onion into four wedges and put them in the bottom of a Dutch oven.
3. Generously salt and pepper the pork roast, then set it on top of the onions in the pan.
4. Pour the can of chipotle peppers and sauce over the pork. Pour in both cans of Dr Pepper. Stir the brown sugar into the liquid.
5. Cover the pot tightly, then set the pot in the oven. Cook the meat for 6 hours, flipping the meat over every hour and a half. If the meat is not falling apart after 6 hours, cook it for another hour.
6. Remove the meat from the liquid and shred it with two forks. Strain the liquid, then place the liquid in the freezer until the fat on top freezes. Scrape off the fat, heat the liquid in the microwave till steaming, and pour it over the meat.

## PULLED PORK

This recipe is my wife's most requested dish. Evelyn eats it, too. Gunnar only eats bacon, but that's another story. I cook this on a Big Green Egg. It can feed an army and is super, super simple.

1 (5- to 7-pound) bone-in pork shoulder (also known as Boston butt)

## INJECTION
½ cup sugar
¼ cup kosher salt
½ cup hot water
¾ cup cold apple juice, plus ½ cup for the smoker
2 tablespoons Worcestershire sauce
1 tablespoon Louisiana hot sauce
1 teaspoon freshly ground black pepper

## RUB
½ cup turbinado sugar (Sugar in the Raw)
½ cup kosher salt
3 tablespoons chili powder
3 tablespoons smoked paprika
1 teaspoon garlic powder
1 teaspoon onion powder
½ teaspoon freshly ground black pepper
½ teaspoon lemon pepper
¼ teaspoon cayenne pepper

1. To make the injection, dissolve the sugar and salt in the hot water. Add the ¾ cup apple juice, Worcestershire, hot sauce, and pepper. Whisk to dissolve any undissolved salt and sugar. Inject the meat and let it stand in the refrigerator for at least 1 hour.

2. Rub oil (or yellow mustard) lightly on the meat after it has been sitting in the fridge for an hour post-injection. Mix together all the rub ingredients. Pack the rub all over the meat and work it into the crevices.

3. Put the pork on a smoker set for 235° to 240°F, with water filled in the drip pan. When the meat gets to 170°F, put it in an aluminum foil pan covered tightly or wrapped tightly in two layers of heavy-duty aluminum foil, with ½ cup of apple juice added before sealing.

4. Get the meat to 205°F. Let it rest for an hour before pulling. Pour out the juices into a tall measuring cup and place in the freezer to let the fat rise to the top and solidify. Scrape off the fat, heat the remaining liquid in the microwave till hot, and pour over the meat. The total cooking time can be up to 15 hours, but the meat will fall off the bone and easily shred.

Note: I recommend using half hickory wood chips and half applewood chips.

## BRISKET

This is where marriage gets complicated. Christy is from Georgia and in Georgia they eat pigs for barbecue. I am from Louisiana by way of Dubai and I grew up eating beef for barbecue. Normally, when I make Christy pulled pork, I put this on afterward. The brisket usually cooks in four to six hours. Thankfully, Christy's dad will help me eat this. The key is to be light with the rub. I pack it in on the pulled pork, but go light on the brisket. I think brisket is more flavorful than pulled pork anyway.

1 (5-pound or more) brisket
4 cups beef broth
2 tablespoons Worcestershire sauce
1 tablespoon Louisiana hot sauce
½ cup kosher salt
¼ cup turbinado sugar (Sugar in the Raw)
1 tablespoon freshly ground black pepper

1. Trim the fat from the brisket. Doesn't have to be thorough, just make sure the fat is not too thick. Mix the broth, Worcestershire, and hot sauce together and inject the brisket thoroughly. You won't use all the liquid. Let the brisket rest on the counter for an hour, which will also bring it up in temperature a bit.
2. Rub the brisket lightly with oil. Mix the salt, sugar, and pepper together and sprinkle the rub on lightly. Don't pack it in. You'll have some left over.
3. Put the brisket on a smoker set for 235°

to 240°F with water filled in the drip pan. When the meat gets to 170°F, wrap it in heavy-duty aluminum foil or, preferably, butcher paper, and keep smoking it until the temperature reaches 205°F.
4. If I want it done faster, I'll raise the smoker's heat as high as 275°F, but never higher than that.

Note: I use oak wood when I make brisket.

## BRISKET SAUCE

I sometimes put pictures on Instagram of what I am cooking, and there is always some jerk who is outraged that I would put sauce on my brisket. "You aren't cooking it right if you use a sauce," the jerk will say. My reply is that if he tasted my sauce, he would understand why. The brisket, delicious by itself, is a vehicle for this most excellent sauce. I found a recipe in a cookbook put out by Williams-Sonoma, but I altered it to get the citrusy-sweet flavor profile that I love. If you try only one recipe, try this. It is great on burgers, chicken, brisket, steak, you name it.

2 tablespoons margarine (Don't use
   butter. Trust me.)
½ sweet or yellow onion, finely chopped
1 clove garlic, minced
1 cup Heinz ketchup

⅓ cup fresh lemon juice
¼ cup packed light brown sugar
2 tablespoons honey
1 tablespoon Worcestershire sauce
1 tablespoon yellow mustard

In a small saucepan, melt the margarine over medium heat, then add the onion. Stir the onion until it is brown, about 20 minutes. Add the garlic and stir for 1 minute. Add the remaining ingredients and bring to a boil. Reduce the heat to low and simmer, stirring occasionally, until thickened, 15 to 20 minutes. Use immediately or refrigerate in an airtight container for up to 2 weeks.

## BARBECUE BEEF PO'BOYS

During my youth, we would return to Louisiana during the summers. There was a fine-dining restaurant in my hometown called Bear Corners. During the day, the restaurant served sandwiches, one of which was a barbecue beef po'boy. It was divine. The recipe was common to the area. When I was in high school, my brother-in-law would pick up these po'boys from a gas station in Woodville, Mississippi. They were spicy, sweet, and wonderful. I have yet to find the exact recipe, but I stumbled across a book by a man who drove the backroads of

Louisiana collecting po'boy recipes. I took one of his as a base and got it as close as I can to the taste I remember. When my family comes for Thanksgiving every year, this has to be made.

1 (4- to 5-pound) brisket
1½ cups cold water
3 tablespoons Worcestershire sauce
2 tablespoons apple cider vinegar
2 cloves garlic, minced
2 teaspoons beef bouillon granules
1½ teaspoons chili powder
1 teaspoon ground mustard
½ teaspoon cayenne pepper
½ teaspoon garlic salt

## SAUCE

1 cup ketchup
¼ cup brown sugar
2 tablespoons unsalted butter
1 tablespoon Louisiana hot sauce

1. Preheat the oven to 300°F.
2. Place the brisket in a large Dutch oven. In a small bowl, whisk together the water, Worcestershire sauce, vinegar, garlic, bouillon, chili powder, mustard, cayenne, and garlic salt. Reserve ½ cup of the mixture in the fridge. Pour the remainder over the beef.

3. Cover and cook for 4 hours, until the meat falls apart.
4. Remove the beef and skim the fat from the cooking juices. Remove the fat from the beef. Shred the meat and return it to the Dutch oven to heat through with the juices.
5. In a small saucepan, combine the sauce ingredients and reserved ½ cup mixture. Bring to a boil over medium-high heat, then reduce the heat to low. Simmer for 25 minutes. Pour over the meat. Split a French bread in half, slather on some mayo, add this meat, and enjoy a bit of my childhood.

## BRAISED SHORT RIBS

This is another recipe inspired by the Pioneer Woman. My friend Dave Bufkin made osso buco one time for a dinner I attended. It was amazing and I have been craving it ever since. But one of the downsides of living in Macon, Georgia, is that I cannot find veal shanks anywhere. I stumbled across an osso buco recipe with short ribs from the Pioneer Woman and set about merging bits and pieces of it with Dave's recipe. One thing I have since discovered is that it works great with a regular old beef roast, too. And I have started using boneless short ribs because Christy likes their texture better.

8 beef short ribs
Kosher salt
Freshly ground black pepper
½ cup all-purpose flour
3 tablespoons bacon drippings
1 tablespoon vegetable oil
1 medium onion, diced
3 carrots, diced
2 cups beef broth (or red wine if you
   must, but grapes are disgusting)
2 cups chicken stock
2 thyme sprigs
2 rosemary sprigs

1. Preheat the oven to 350°F.
2. Salt and pepper the ribs, then dredge them in the flour.
3. In a large Dutch oven, heat the bacon drippings over medium-high heat until they have turned liquid and are hot. Add the oil. Brown the ribs on all sides, about 45 seconds per side. Remove the ribs and set aside. Turn the heat to medium.
4. Add the onion and carrots to the pan and cook for 2 minutes. Pour in the beef broth and scrape the bottom of the pan to release all the stuck bits of deliciousness. Bring to a boil and cook for 2 minutes.
5. Add the chicken stock and season with salt and pepper. Add the ribs; they should

be almost completely submerged. Add the thyme and rosemary sprigs to the liquid.

6. Cover the pot and place it in the oven. Cook for 2 hours, then reduce the oven temperature to 325°F and cook for an additional 45 minutes. The ribs should be fork-tender and falling off the bone. Remove the pot from the oven and allow to sit for at least 20 minutes, lid on, before serving. At the last minute, skim the fat off the top of the liquid.

7. I serve the ribs on top of mashed potatoes and spoon the juices over the potatoes.

## CORNFLAKE CHICKEN

This recipe is the first thing I ever cooked for Christy, and she makes me cook it for our anniversary, her birthday, and at other random times. I have no idea why, but she loves it. It is the first dish I ever truly mastered as a kid. I've served it to WWF wrestlers, visiting preachers, family, and friends. It is a regular in our home and has been a regular in my home since I was eight years old. Even my dad, who hates chicken, eats it.

4 cups cornflakes
½ cup (1 stick) unsalted butter
2 tablespoons Cajun seasoning
4 to 6 boneless, skinless chicken breasts

1. Preheat the oven to 350°F. Grease a casserole dish large enough to hold the number of chicken breasts you are preparing.
2. Place the cornflakes in a gallon-size Ziplock bag and smash them to bits. Place the butter in a bowl, cover in the Cajun seasoning, and melt in a microwave. Dip the chicken breasts in the butter, then in the cornflakes, then place in the casserole dish. Cover with the excess cornflakes. Pour the remaining butter and seasoning on top of the cornflakes. Bake for 1 hour.

## NATCHITOCHES MEAT PIES

This is a taste of home, and I have *Garden & Gun* magazine to thank for this recipe. North and South Louisiana are like two different countries on the far sides of the world from each other. But they all love to eat. This is "Yankee food" to my South Louisiana friends, but the trinity of bell pepper, onion, and celery is still there.

### FOR THE DOUGH

2¼ cups all-purpose flour
1½ teaspoons kosher salt
½ teaspoon baking powder
½ cup (1 stick) unsalted butter, cut into small pieces and placed in the freezer

1 large egg
½ cup ice water
2 teaspoons distilled white vinegar

## FOR THE FILLING
1 teaspoon olive oil
½ pound ground chuck
½ pound ground pork
½ cup finely chopped green bell pepper
½ cup finely chopped yellow onion
½ cup finely chopped celery
2 garlic cloves, minced
½ teaspoon kosher salt
¼ teaspoon freshly ground black pepper
Pinch of cayenne pepper
1 bay leaf
½ teaspoon Worcestershire sauce
1 cup beef broth
2 teaspoons all-purpose flour
1 large egg whisked with 1 tablespoon
   water

1. Make the dough: Put the flour, salt, and baking powder in a food processor and pulse three times. Scatter the pieces of frozen butter and pulse until everything comes together in pea-size bits. In a bowl, whisk together the egg, water, and vinegar, then add it to the flour and pulse to form a shaggy dough.

2. Put the dough between two sheets of plastic wrap and knead a few times, shape into a disk, wrap tight, and place in the refrigerator for 1 hour.
3. Meanwhile, make the filling: Heat the oil in a skillet over medium-high heat and cook the meat thoroughly, breaking it apart. Let the moisture evaporate, then reduce the heat to medium and add the trinity, plus the garlic. Cook for 10 minutes.
4. Add the salt, black pepper, cayenne, and bay leaf. Combine the Worcestershire sauce and beef broth, then pour half of that into the skillet. Scrape the bottom to get all the bits off the skillet. Let the liquid evaporate, stirring frequently. Whisk the flour into the remaining broth mixture, then add that to the skillet and cook for 5 minutes. Remove from the heat. Remove the bay leaf.
5. Preheat the oven to 400°F.
6. Remove the dough from the refrigerator and divide it into twelve equal portions. Roll each into a 6-inch disk less than ¼ inch thick.
7. To make each pie, place 2 tablespoons of meat on the bottom portion of a dough round. Dip your finger in the egg wash, then paint around the edge of the circle.

Fold the dough over in half, then press to seal the edges. Cut two slits in the top, brush with the remaining egg wash, then place on a parchment-lined baking sheet. Bake for 30 minutes or until golden brown.

Note: These can be frozen once assembled, then thawed in the fridge for 3 hours before baking.

## PASTA SHELL TACOS

When Christy was pregnant with Evelyn, she belonged to a knitting group called "Stitch & Bitch," which describes what they did. The office manager of my law firm, Carlene Massey, had gotten Christy into knitting as a social outlet. Carlene made this dish one night and suddenly, throughout Christy's pregnancy, she wanted it all the time. It is quite delicious and we make it regularly. We often stuff the shells and cover the pan and freeze them. It makes a great meal to give to friends. Christy does not like spicy stuff as much as I do, so we tend to divide the taco sauce between a mild and medium variety.

18 jumbo pasta shells
2 tablespoons unsalted butter, melted
1¼ pounds ground chuck

4 ounces cream cheese
1 teaspoon salt
1 teaspoon chili powder
1 cup taco sauce
2 cups shredded Mexican blend cheese
1½ cups crushed tortilla chips

1. Preheat the oven to 350°F. Grease a 9 x 13-inch baking dish.
2. Bring a large pot of lightly salted water to a boil. Add the pasta and cook until al dente, 8 to 10 minutes, then drain. Toss the cooked shells in the melted butter.
3. Meanwhile, in a large skillet, brown the beef over medium heat until no longer pink; drain. Add the cream cheese, salt, and chili powder. Mix together and simmer for 5 minutes.
4. Fill the shells with the beef mixture and arrange in the prepared baking dish; pour the taco sauce over the stuffed shells. Cover with aluminum foil and bake for 15 minutes. Remove the dish from the oven, remove the foil, and top with the cheese and crushed tortilla chips. Return the dish to the oven, uncovered, for 15 more minutes to melt and brown the cheese.

# RED BEANS AND RICE

We eat this almost every Monday night. It is my mother's recipe. Every family in Louisiana has its own. This is ours and I love it.

½ cup vegetable oil (or bacon drippings
   for more flavorful beans)
3 green onions, chopped
½ yellow onion, chopped
1 clove garlic, minced
½ teaspoon salt
½ teaspoon freshly ground black pepper
¼ teaspoon cayenne pepper
2 bay leaves
1 (16-ounce) can dark kidney beans
1 (16-ounce) can light kidney beans
4 cups water
2 cups rice

1. Heat the oil in a large pot over medium heat. Add the green onions and yellow onion. Stir till wilted and browning. Add the garlic and stir until it browns. Add the salt, black pepper, cayenne, and bay leaves. Stir together. Add the beans with their liquid.

2. Pour water into one of the cans, filling it no more than halfway. Swirl the water around in the can to get the bean residue and pour it into the pot. Stir. Bring to a

boil and stir. Reduce to a simmer and stir occasionally to prevent sticking.

3. In a large saucepan, bring the water to a boil over high heat and add the rice. Reduce the heat to low, cover, and cook, undisturbed, for 20 minutes. When the rice is done, the beans are done. Remove the bay leaves.

Note: If you like, thinly slice andouille sausage, then brown it in the pot. Remove the sausage and use the drippings instead of the oil. Add the sausage back to the pot to reheat after the beans are done.

# THANKSGIVING

Evelyn and Gunnar, here are the brine, turkey, and gravy recipes I use every year.

### TURKEY BRINE

I agree with the Pioneer Woman: This is my favorite turkey brine recipe. It is genuinely fantastic and makes the house smell wonderful, or at least I think so. Christy finally confessed last year that she didn't really like the smell, but she loves the taste of the turkey. Don't use this if you buy a frozen, pre-brined turkey. But if you get a fresh turkey, use this.

1 gallon water
3 cups apple juice or apple cider

2 cups brown sugar
Peel of 3 large oranges
¼ cup fresh rosemary leaves
5 cloves garlic, minced
1½ cups kosher salt
3 tablespoons whole black peppercorns
5 bay leaves

Combine all the ingredients in a big pot and bring to a boil. Stir to dissolve the salt and sugar. Then scoop in lots of ice to cool it down, up to a gallon extra of water because of the ice you'll use. Set a turkey (with the innards removed) in a brining bag, pour the chilled brine over it, and brine overnight in the fridge or in a cooler of ice. Next morning, discard the brine and rinse the turkey thoroughly before use.

## SMOKED TURKEY

The first year I was at CNN, I bought a Big Green Egg. The first time I used the Big Green Egg, I grilled hamburgers. In fact, it was the day before I flew to Washington, DC, to be on set during the president's State of the Union address. The damn thing got so hot, when I opened it I burned off my eyebrows, the hair on my fingers, and the front bit of hair on my freshly cut head. I went into the bathroom and could smell burned hair. I looked in the mirror and suddenly realized why. I do believe I dropped an F-bomb. (Sorry, kids.) Now I mostly use the Egg for smoking things, because Christy does not care for the flavor of charcoal. I have a gigantic DCS grill for grilling and the Egg for smoking. The first Thanksgiving after I got the Egg, I smoked a turkey, which is normally my father-in-law's job. Now I find I am charged with smoking a turkey every year. I use the brine above and this recipe.

1 chicken
1 turkey
2 yellow onions, halved, divided
2 stalks celery, halved lengthwise
2 carrots, chopped
1 bunch tarragon sprigs, divided
1 bunch thyme sprigs, divided
1 bunch rosemary sprigs, divided
Salt
Freshly ground black pepper
1 apple, quartered
1 lemon, quartered
1 clove garlic, peeled (optional)
3 sticks unsalted butter, at room
   temperature

1. Put the whole chicken and the turkey neck in a large stockpot. Add 1 halved onion, the celery, carrots, and half

of each herb. Fill the pot with water. Simmer for at least 6 hours. Strain. Toss the neck, save the chicken meat for post-Thanksgiving gumbo, and save the broth for the gravy.

2. Rinse the turkey, then pat dry; add salt and pepper to the cavity fairly liberally. Into the cavity stick the remaining halved onion, the apple, lemon, and the remaining herbs (if you are a garlic person, it's a good place to stick that as well). Smear the turkey all over with 2 sticks of the butter. Place the remaining stick of butter in the cavity.

3. Put the bird in a V-rack, breast side up, and fold the wings under the front of the bird. About 20 minutes before you put it in the Egg, fill a gallon-size Ziplock bag with ice cubes and lay it over the breasts for the 20 minutes.

4. Bring the Big Green Egg up to 300°F for at least 45 minutes before putting the turkey in. Fill a drip pan with water. Insert the turkey. Cover it loosely with aluminum foil if it gets too brown. The turkey is done when a thermometer reads 180°F in the thigh and 160°F in the breast.

Note: I use pecan wood when I smoke the turkey.

# HOMEMADE GRAVY

I am horrified by people who use canned gravy. It is an abomination and a crime against the universe. Gravy is easy to make if you spend time making cooking love to your onions. In another life, Ina Garten would be my goddess and muse. The woman is amazing and everything she cooks is amazing, even when I'm disgusted by the ingredients. There are so many celebrity chefs out there, and I love that she is so unpretentious. The woman just loves her husband and loves to cook and loves Paris. If I ever have my cooking show, she and Ree Drummond will join me to make gumbo, chocolate pie, and bread. I am mentioning Ina Garten because I learned to make gravy by watching her. This recipe is based on one she used on her TV show. My entire family expects this gravy at Thanksgiving. We do not eat until it is done.

½ cup (1 stick) unsalted butter
1 medium sweet onion, finely chopped
¼ cup all-purpose flour
1 teaspoon kosher salt
½ teaspoon freshly ground black pepper
2 cups stock made with chicken and
　　turkey neck (see page 215), heated
1 tablespoon heavy cream

1.　In a 10- to 12-inch skillet, melt the butter over medium heat and cook the onions for

20 to 30 minutes, or until the onions are nicely brown. Take your time with this. It is the secret to amazing gravy.

2. Sprinkle the flour into the pan, whisk well, then add the salt and pepper. Cook for 3 minutes, whisking occasionally. Add the hot stock and cook, uncovered, for 4 to 5 minutes, or until thickened. Add the cream. Season to taste, and serve.

Note: You can brown the onions the day before in the butter, then store them in a jar in a fridge. Reheat in a skillet till bubbling on Thanksgiving Day before adding the flour.

# DESSERTS

I am twice the man I was before I was married, literally. Christy lured me in with homemade buttermilk biscuits, then kept me trained with pound cake and chocolate pie. Now these are our kids' favorites, too, though we try to have them only in moderation.

## CHOCOLATE PIE

I blame the Pioneer Woman for this recipe and for my waistline. I can't blame my wife, really. I also blame her for this recipe. Note that it uses raw eggs, and the pie should be kept refrigerated. Wait, who am I kidding? There will be nothing to keep. The last time I made this pie, my sisters and brothers-in-law stood over it as I was making it. It never even made it to the chill part. It simply disappeared. I had to make another one.

1 deep-dish pie shell
4 ounces unsweetened baking chocolate
1 cup (2 sticks) salted butter, at room
  temperature
1½ cups sugar
1 teaspoon vanilla extract
4 large eggs
Whipped cream

1. Bake the pie shell according to the package instructions and set aside to cool to room temperature.
2. In a small microwave-safe bowl, melt the chocolate for about 45 seconds, until it can be stirred. Set aside to cool.
3. In the bowl of a mixer fitted with the whisk attachment, cream the butter and sugar for 2 minutes. When the melted chocolate is cooled, drizzle it over the butter while the mixer is on low speed. Add the vanilla. Whisk until thoroughly combined.
4. Turn your mixer to medium speed and over 20 minutes add the eggs, one at a time, leaving about 5 minutes between

each egg. Once the pie filling is well mixed, pour it into the baked pie shell. Chill for at least 3 hours before serving. Serve with whipped cream, which balances out the sweetness perfectly.

## BUTTERMILK PIE

This is the pie of true community. Our pastor Chip Miller and his wife, Barbara, frequently invite church members over to their house for lunch on Sundays. I don't know how Barbara does it, but she prepares these fantastic meals and everyone gets to telling stories and enjoying the day. One time, Barbara served up this pie. I had never had it before, and because of the way it browns on top, I presumed it was the disgusting coconut pie Christy likes. I am opposed to coconut because it is like eating hair. Still, because my mama taught me good manners and Christy was glaring at me, I took a bite. I cannot swear to it, but I am pretty sure the clouds parted, a band of angels descended singing hallelujahs, and we had a new favorite pie. It is crazy simple. There is one catch: Use whole buttermilk. God will smite me and your pie will turn out to be garbage if you use low-fat buttermilk.

½ cup (1 stick) unsalted butter, melted
   and slightly cooled
1½ cups sugar

2 tablespoons all-purpose flour
3 large eggs
½ cup buttermilk
2 teaspoons vanilla extract
1 deep-dish or regular pie shell

1. Preheat the oven to 350°F.
2. In a large bowl, beat the melted butter, sugar, and flour with a hand mixer. Add the eggs and beat some more. Add the buttermilk and vanilla. Mix thoroughly. Pour into an unbaked pie shell. Bake for 40 minutes, or until browned and set. It will get a brown crust on top.

Note: Here's a variation that I hate and Christy loves: Add the grated zest of 1 lemon and sprinkle in blueberries. This takes longer to cook and I have no idea how long because I am horrified by the very idea of this.

## DAD'S CHOCOLATE CHIP COOKIES

Christy and I are always on the hunt for a recipe for a chocolate chip cookie that is crisp at the edges and chewy in the middle and that does not dry out overnight, assuming they last that long. The kids love to eat the cookie dough without it ever getting baked. I love these cookies. You can also chop up a cup of pecans or walnuts and toss into the dough at the end. The secret to this dough is cornstarch. Cornstarch and brown sugar work in concert to make the dough hygroscopic, which is a fancy way of saying it attracts moisture and does not dry out so quickly.

¾ cup (1½ sticks) unsalted butter
2 cups plus 2 tablespoons all-purpose flour
2 tablespoons cornstarch
1 teaspoon baking soda
½ teaspoon salt
1 cup brown sugar
½ cup granulated sugar
2 large eggs
1 tablespoon vanilla extract
Dash of almond extract (optional)
11 to 12 ounces chocolate chips (I use
  milk chocolate, but semisweet works.)

1. Melt the butter in the microwave and set aside to cool to room temperature.
2. Sift the flour, cornstarch, baking soda, and salt into a small mixing bowl. Set aside.
3. When the butter is cooled, add it to the bowl of an electric mixer fitted with the whisk attachment. Add the brown sugar and granulated sugar. Cream for 1 minute on medium speed. Beat in the eggs and vanilla. Add the almond extract, if using.

4. Add the flour mixture to the butter and sugar mixture. Mix until well combined. Stir in the chocolate chips.
5. Cover the dough and chill for at least 1 hour—the longer, the better.
6. Preheat the oven to 325°F.
7. Scoop the dough and place on a parchment-lined baking sheet 2 inches apart. Bake for 10 to 12 minutes, or until the edges are brown and the centers are still soft.

## POUND CAKE

When Gunnar was little, he knew he was not supposed to have cake for breakfast, so he would ask for "that thing that looks like bread, but isn't." If he asked for cake, he was not getting it, but in his mind if he went for bread he'd be able to get his hands on it. That would be this pound cake. Christy has made several versions over the years and has finally settled on this one. I now make it when she does not have time. Amazingly, the kids like it when I make it. One key is to lightly grease and flour the Bundt pan. You want enough so that the cake does not stick, but not so much that it cannot rise up the edges. I cannot remember where Christy got this recipe. I think it was in some book the local Junior League was handing out for free at the grocery store. Regardless, this is a winner.

1 cup (2 sticks) salted butter, at room temperature
3 cups sugar
3 cups all-purpose flour
¼ teaspoon baking soda
Pinch of salt
6 large eggs, at room temperature
8 ounces sour cream, at room temperature
1 teaspoon vanilla extract
1 teaspoon almond extract

1. Preheat the oven to 300°F. Grease and flour a Bundt pan.
2. Put the butter in the bowl of an electric mixer fitted with the paddle attachment, set it to medium speed, then add the sugar. Cream the mixture, stopping occasionally to scrape down the sides of the bowl.
3. While the mixture is creaming, lay out two sheets of wax paper. Sift the flour onto the first sheet. Then, scoop 3 level, unpacked cups of the sifted flour from the first sheet and place on the second sheet. (You will not use the remaining flour on the first sheet.) Add the baking soda and salt to the flour, then sift it all into a bowl and set aside.
4. Separate each egg, putting all the whites in a bowl and adding the yolks to the butter mixture. After each yolk is added

to the batter, mix thoroughly. Add the sour cream and flour mixture, a third at a time, alternating between the two and mixing well between each addition. Add the vanilla and almond extracts.

5. Beat the egg whites until stiff peaks form, then fold the egg whites into the batter. It is okay to use the paddle attachment to mix in stiffly beaten egg whites, but you can fold them in by hand if you are paranoid. Pour the batter into the prepared Bundt pan.

6. Bake for 90 minutes. Try to minimize loud sounds and vibrations while the cake is baking, or else this one really will fall. It is very unstable until it is baked.

7. Remove from the oven and let rest in the pan for 10 minutes. Turn out onto a plate and then quickly turn it over again onto a cake platter so that the crunchy crust is on top.

# • TEN •
# LAGNIAPPE

Lagniappe is pronounced "lan-yap" and is a word from South Louisiana. It means "a little something extra." If I ever opened a restaurant, I'd call it Lagniappe, even though I would have to train the staff for a month on how to pronounce it.

I have lots of things I would want Gunnar and Evelyn to know if I were to die in the night. I would want them to know our favorite family recipes. I would want them to know about God, life, me, why they need to travel, how they need to be aware that others shape them, why they must build community, and I would want them to know a lot of simple, little things that are not, in and of themselves, worth a full chapter. But together they are useful. I know these things are true and I know my children will come to know them as well. Here's some lagniappe:

~

Turn your clothes right side out, especially your socks. Your mom hates it when you don't, even if she doesn't tell you.

Nobody can figure out the little symbols on laundry. Separate out the whites from the darks and wash new stuff in cold water and dry on low heat and you should be good.

~

Change your pillow every year and your mattress every decade.

~

Do not keep company with people who can never admit they were wrong.

~

Always say please and thank you, but never expect others to reciprocate.

~

Learn to bake bread. The smell of yeasty dough is a smell that soothes the soul and makes a house feel like home.

~

When you get married, move at least a day's drive from home so you cannot always run home to Mom when you hit a rough patch.

~

Get married and stay married. Remember, happiness is not the goal of marriage. Happiness is the by-product of marriage. The goal of marriage is for two people to become one in body and one in mind.

~

Find a good babysitter. Have a date night. Your mom and I suck at this. Do better.

Buy a paper road atlas. Learn to read it.

~

Your kitchen is not your living room.

~

Batman is the best superhero because he is not super. He is smart. Superman is boring.

~

Your Ampaw likes to say, "An eagle may soar, but a weasel never gets sucked up in a jet engine."

~

Laugh, but don't be a weasel.

~

Learn to handle a gun.

~

Learn to flip an omelet. Cook.

~

Have friends over and do all the cooking. You'd be amazed how few people do this these days.

~

Flush and put the seat down.

~

Learn a foreign language and travel to that country.

~

Always have one friend who can
tell you when you've screwed up.
Surrounding yourself
with yes men will ruin you.
When you come home at the end of the day,

hug your children, pet your dog, but give
the longest kiss to your spouse. Your spouse
is meant to be with you forever. The kids
will eventually move out.

~

Pumpkins are gourds, not spices. People who
like pumpkin spice are weird.

~

Print your best photographs. Delete your worst.
The digital age lets us accumulate so many
memories on computers, but we forget to print
them out. Photographic memories are art. They
capture life as it was for a fleeting moment. Print
out those pictures, share them, savor them, and
smile at them. Do not let them collect digital
dust, forgotten on some old computer.

~

If you cannot find any criticism of your
employer, you have drunk the Kool-Aid. Nobody
is perfect and no company is perfect. When you
can no longer offer constructive criticism, you
can no longer be useful to friends and employers.

~

Learn to enjoy dark chocolate. It is good for your
heart. But it is an acquired taste.

~

Eat sweet potatoes.

~

Understand that there are beautiful things you
may not like. Be able to appreciate their beauty

even though you do not personally like them. Beethoven's music is beautiful even if it is not your favorite.

~

Fathers do not know everything, but when our children are little they think we know everything and are amazed by every utterance. It is during this time that we shape our children for later in life. If we lie, they will lie. If we are honest, they will be honest.

~

Wherever you are, leave a place in better condition than you found it. A public restroom is the major exception here. Touch nothing in a public restroom. But your home, your school, your community, and your planet should be improved. Note, however, that in leaving places better than you found them, there will always be those who think you are doing harm or doing wrong.

~

Life is not fair, nor was it ever meant to be.

~

Equality of people does not and cannot guarantee equality of outcomes.

~

We are all born equal into the world, but we do not all have the same opportunities. Never feel guilty for the opportunities you have had and never be jealous or envious of the opportunities you missed out on. When people talk negatively about "privilege," what they really mean is that you benefited from a two-parent nuclear household and should feel guilty about it. Don't. They're trying to rationalize themselves as a victim.

~

People are sinners. They are bound to disappoint. Forgive them when they do, but never expect to be forgiven.

~

Salvation may be by faith alone, but judgment is based on works. Leave the world better than you found it. Just remember that the world's definition of better is oftentimes not God's.

~

Take care of widows, orphans, the poor, and refugees. God commands it, not your dad. Your personal obligation to care for the widows, the orphans, the poor, and the refugees cannot be abdicated and passed off to government. You have an obligation to help them because God says so. If you cannot give money, give time.

~

Never fully trust someone who thinks the Bible is only legitimate in the King James Version.

~

The Bible is prose, poetry, prophecy, history, and apocalyptic in parts. Know which is which and read them the same way. Even those of us who accept the Bible as literal understand that not everything in the Bible is literally so.

~

Salvation may be through grace, but there are oughts—things you ought to do. Failing to do them does not mean you will lose your salvation, but it might suggest you never had it to begin with.

~

Breaking the law is a sin, but driving right at the speed limit is annoying. God will forgive you for modestly exceeding it. But the police officer might not.

~

The closer art gets to the divine, the more it is art. The further away from the divine you go, the closer you eventually get to a toilet seat nailed to a wall with a bunch of skinny-jean-wearing hipsters applauding it as bold. It is not bold. It is stupid.

~

Apologize. Have an accountability group who can be honest with you and you with them and who can push you to be better than who you are.

~

Sometimes when you think people are not practicing what they preach, they are preaching because they failed to practice it and realize they were wrong.

Sometimes you do have to turn off your phone and spend time with your family. Yes, I preach this because I realize how many times I have failed to practice it.

~

Stand up for those who cannot stand up for themselves. Pray for those in need. Try to spend more time in prayer thanking God for his blessings than asking him for your wants.

~

Repent.

~

Everyone worships something and everyone has a god. Who our god is defines what we worship and how we minister to others. Even atheists have a god. The question is whether you worship the real God of heaven and earth or an idol. What you put first in life is probably your god. Money is rarely a person's god, but what that money goes toward can often reveal it.

~

Tithe and give money to church.
God does not need your money,
but your money does need God.

~

The gospel message does not offer wealth, health, and prosperity. Christianity is a religion of persecution and suffering. Sometimes Christians succeed and do well, but of them God expects much. When anyone tells you

Christianity will make you rich,
go the other way.

~

If you have never experienced even some small
measure of persecution, you might need to assess
the sincerity of your faith.

~

You never have to worry about forgetting the
truth, but you always have to remember the lie.

~

There are those who through physical or mental
defect are unable to help themselves. You are
obligated to take care of them.

~

Do not try to make a poor person comfortable in
their poverty. Work to elevate the person out of
poverty. We may always have the poor, but we
need not always have the same person poor.

~

In the internet age, privacy is platinum. Some
things are meant to stay private.

~

Everybody and everything needs a Sabbath
rest.

~

Trends come and go, but classics are forever.
If you dress in trendy clothes, at some point
you'll find yourself out of fashion.
Dress like a normal person and you'll never
have to worry about keeping up with the trends.

Classic styles are always stylish and double-breasted suits are for mobsters.

~

Read *The Iliad*. *The Iliad* was originally an oral history passed down from generation to generation, then Homer worked his magic. Thousands of years after the events, based on the story, Heinrich Schliemann found the gates of Troy. If the basic facts of an oral history could hold up over thousands of years, why couldn't the Exodus have happened or the resurrection?

~

Don't settle for just *The Iliad*. The canon of Western civilization is rich, broad, and necessary for a well-developed mind. But the politics of the twenty-first century would tell you it's all a bunch of patriarchal dead white men. Nonsense. Nonetheless, the dead patriarchal white men are the ones who shaped history, carved up the map, and charted the world into modernity. Just because some people fall out of favor with the zeitgeist, that does not mean they should truly be dismissed.

~

Evil is real. Truth is truth. Morality is not relative. God is real.

~

Reality TV will rot your brain.

~

Live in the moment instead of simply trying to document it all on your cell phone's camera.

Some ideas are worth fighting for.

~

When you never find conflict between God and your politics, politics has become your God.

~

Clickbait is trash that cheapens
the experience of reading.
Seek out people who write well
and thoughtfully.

~

They say it is the thought that counts, but some gifts clearly indicate you weren't thinking.

~

"I feel" is not equivalent to "I think."

~

Don't doubt God. Always doubt people. People are fallible. God is infallible.

~

Some questions have no answers. Some questions need not be answered.

~

"Because I'm Dad," is always a valid response to the question "Why?" The only better response is "Because I'm Batman," but only Batman gets to use that one.

~

You're just passing through this world. The eternal should come first, but the eternal requires engagement with the world. You cannot fully retreat from the world.

Be in the world, but not of the world. Engage the world, but do not become worldly. Be a good steward of the world's resources.

~

Never identify the nation in which you live as heaven-sent. Confusing the nation and the Kingdom will lead you on paths of idolatry.

~

God raises people up for his purposes. You do not have to vote for them. God is big enough to put them where he wants them without you getting your hands dirty.

~

We are all sinners. The smaller the government, the fewer the sinners in charge of you. The larger the government . . .

~

Darth Vader twice lost a Death Star to a ragtag group of rebels. But popular culture remembers him as a badass. Sometimes people get it wrong.

~

Don't do drugs. There are people who will tell you marijuana is not addictive, but ask them to stop using it and watch their reaction.

~

People rush ahead of science. When people say "science says," often they really mean "What I want science to say is . . ."

Science requires hypothesis and testing.
Do the tests enough with each one confirming
your hypothesis and you have a theory.
Someone may come along later and upend it all.

~

Baking is chemistry, which itself is science.
Take so many grams of flour, so many milliliters
of water, throw in some salt, yeast, and sugar
and you have bread every time. But the
measurements come with patience and work
ethic, heavy on the patience.

~

Work gives people meaning and feeds the soul.
In the Garden of Eden, God told Adam and Eve
to tend the garden. They had jobs, even in the
place on earth closest to heaven. Work gives us
meaning. Work gives us purpose. When people
do not work, they lose meaning. It is better to
work for only a little money than to never work
for a lot of money.

~

Inherited wealth is usually squandered by
the third generation. I saw it while a lawyer.
Grandfather worked hard to make a business;
the father took over the business without
appreciating the sweat equity his father put into
it; the son comes along and has no appreciation
at all for it and screws it up.

~

Avoid doing business with your family. If you
ever loan a family member money, treat it as a

gift and be delightfully surprised
if it is ever repaid.

~

As long as you are financially dependent on your
parents, yes, they do get to set rules for your
existence.

~

Love is a verb, not a noun. It requires you to take
some action.

~

A computer is not a substitute for a person.

~

Write letters. Buy stationery, a good pen, and
write. Don't worry about your penmanship. Just
write letters with actual ink, actual paper, and
actual stamps. Nobody does it anymore. That
makes it unique.

~

In the cool of the fall air, make homemade pizza
and pumpkin pie with the kitchen windows
open.

~

Play golf. You may suck at it, but it gets you
outside moving and forces your brain to work.

~

Take long walks alone, turn off the music, and
talk to God. He's ready to listen.

~

Memorize Bible verses. Even if you are reading
this and are not a believer, memorize Bible

verses. The history of Western civilization, our shared idiomatic expressions and colloquialisms, and our foundational storytelling are derived from the Bible. Memorize its verses.

~

With science, you must understand to believe. With faith, you must believe to understand. Neither negates the other. There is a rational basis for faith, just as there is a rational basis for science. Neither explains the other, but both exist. Miracles are outside science, and trying to find science to explain the miracle elevates science above faith. In the same way, dismissing the science of a plane taking off the ground and trusting in God alone to pick it up elevates foolishness above science.

~

G. K. Chesterton was right about the democracy of the dead. "Tradition means giving votes to the most obscure of all classes, our ancestors. It is the democracy of the dead. Tradition refuses to submit to the small and arrogant oligarchy of those who merely happen to be walking about."

~

Listen more than you speak. Observe and ask questions. Understand that you do not know everything and some people do know more than you. Remember that many of the talking heads on television who are "political commentators" have never really done anything in politics

besides lick stamps or sleep with the right
person. Pay attention to resumes.

~

Be humble and always
put the needs of others first.
Hedonism sounds awesome.
But at its root, it is selfishness.

~

Altruism is real and sometimes people really
have no other motive than to want to help.

~

Be comfortable, but never be complacent.

~

If the kids are under your roof, you have every
right and obligation to know what they are
doing, who their friends are, and what they are
doing on the internet. A good parent investigates
and serves as an accountability partner with their
children. A bad parent lets their children run
amok on the internet.

~

Pornography will ruin your relationship.
Adultery is more than just being with another
person physically. You will find that the people
most insistent on telling you how you should live
your married life are people who are either not
faithful or not married.

~

God has a sense of humor.
Have you seen the platypus?

Never trust a Christian
who cannot laugh.

~

People who throw your sins in your
face have many more than you do.

~

"Trust in the Lord with all your heart,
and do not lean on your own understanding.
In all your ways acknowledge him,
and he will make straight your paths.
Be not wise in your own eyes; fear the Lord,
and turn away from evil. It will be healing
to your flesh and refreshment to your bones.
Honor the Lord with your wealth and
with the first fruits of all your produce;
then your barns will be filled with plenty,
and your vats will be bursting with wine.
My son, do not despise the Lord's discipline
or be weary of his reproof, for the Lord
reproves him whom he loves,
as a father the son in whom he delights." —
Proverbs 3:5–12 (ESV)

~

Plant a garden, even if in a pot. It is good for the
body and soul to grow things and eat them.

~

Imported cheese is better than American cheeses
of the same kind because imported cheeses can
be unpasteurized, which makes them less salty
and more tangy.

Sometimes bad things happen. It does not mean God is punishing you or sending you a message. Sometimes bad things just happen. But sometimes God does want to teach you a lesson. Wisdom comes from recognizing the lessons and recognizing that sometimes bad things just happen.

~

It is okay to not care about things that people passionately believe you should care about. You're an individual, not part of a herd.

~

Christianity requires a trinity: God the Father, God the Son, and God the Holy Spirit. This has been settled doctrine for just about two thousand years. People who believe otherwise are not Christians. That is just a fact.

~

Jesus demands you care for the poor, but sometimes people cite passages out of context. There is such a thing as "wrong text, right doctrine." Be understanding when it happens.

~

Jesus spent more time talking about hell and damnation than any other person in the Bible.

~

It is vastly easier to be dismissive of someone than it is to understand them. That does not make it right to dismiss them.

~

The only good snake is a dead snake.

Just because your mother has tattoos, that does not mean you should get them.

~

Know people who drive pickup trucks. Trucks are the most popular vehicles in America. If you don't know someone who drives a pickup truck, it's you, not them, who lives in a bubble.

~

The first piece of advice I always gave clients when I was a political consultant is still some of the best advice I have ever doled out: Know when you are in the minority, even when you think you are right.

~

If you don't believe in God,
you'll believe in anything.

~

Karma and cosmic justice are not real.
The cosmos is indifferent
in the absence of grace,
which overrides everything.

~

Good things happen to bad people and bad things happen to good people. Do not expect fairness in this world and do not expect unfairness in the next.

~

Life in every state and form is precious,
but it is okay and compatible with this
belief to believe that the person who
takes the life of another forfeits his own.

If every hill is worth dying on, you will die quickly. Some hills are worth dying on.

~

Sometimes your kids say cute things and you do not want to correct them. Evelyn, if you were reading this, it really is route guidance, not Ralph, which is why it is okay that Ralph has a girl's voice. Gunnar, it is SUE-NAH-MEE, not TARE-AH-SUE-MEE.

~

There are some people who want to be offended and live in a state of constant offense. There is nothing you can do about those people. There are other people who live to offend. You can avoid being that person. Never seek to offend, even if you sometimes will.

~

Beethoven, Bach, Brahms, Mozart, Chopin, and the like are better than the musical canon of the twentieth century.

~

It is perfectly okay to not get why some people love the Beatles.

~

Calvin Coolidge was right. When you see ten troubles bounding down the road toward you, if you stand still nine of them will bounce off the road before they get to you.
Not every problem has a solution and not every problem needs your solution. Sometimes it is

more helpful to listen than problem-solve. Some people just need to vent.

~

Mary, Queen of Scots feared the prayers of John Knox more than she feared the combined armies of Europe. Prayer is that powerful.

~

Some people will never like you, will hate everything you do, and will criticize you at every opportunity. The only way to make them stop is to conform to what they want, and that is not worth it. It lets them control you. So just ignore them.

~

Instead of trying to cross traffic, it is often massively more convenient to turn right with traffic, then find a place to turn around.

~

Remember, we do not wage war as the world does. The weapons we fight with have the power to demolish strongholds. For our war is not against flesh and blood, but against the spiritual forces of evil. It is God who arms me with strength. He is the God who avenges me . . . who saves me from my enemies. Be strong and courageous. Do not be terrified or discouraged, for the Lord Your God will be with you wherever you go. Do not be afraid of them, for the Lord Your God Himself will fight for you. Let us not grow weary of doing good, for in due season we will reap, if we do not give up. The Lord is my strength, my rock, my fortress, my deliverer, my shield, my stronghold. No weapon forged against you will prosper and you will refute every tongue that accuses you—this is the heritage of the Lord's servants. For the battle is the Lord's. Therefore, put on the full armor of God so that when the day of evil comes, you may be able to stand your ground. And in all these things we are more than conquerors through Him who loves us.

These thoughts, words, recipes, hopes, and aspirations are things I want Evelyn and Gunnar to cherish. Christy and I are going to die one day. We all will. We do not know the future. But I know these are things I want my children to know are true.

I worry more than I ever should about my kids. My mind races to horror stories. Gunnar is headed off to play in the woods. What if he gets lost? What if a snake bites him? Evelyn is going swimming. What if she falls in, hits her head, and drowns? I hope it is natural to be overprotective and overworry and overthink the dangers that lie ahead for our kids. I just want them to love God, love us, and be kind. Most of all, Gunnar and Evelyn, your mother and I love you so much.

We go into your room and watch you sleep. Evelyn, I keep part of the fabric from your favorite stuffed animal in my travel bag and rub it between my hands to remind me of you. Gunnar,

I keep your laugh on my phone so I can listen to it and hear you. I love you. We love you. When the day comes that you can no longer see us face-to-face, we will just be behind the veil of eternity watching and waiting to hold you once again.

# THANKS

There are so many people who need to be thanked. This is like an Academy Awards speech: I know I am going to forget someone.

But, first and foremost, thanks to my wife and children for inspiring me, pushing me to write this, praying for me, and supporting me. I have not let them read any of this while I was writing it, so my apologies in advance if you do not like it. Likewise, my parents, in-laws, and siblings all played a role in shaping me and the stories in this book.

Thanks to Tripp Self, but for whom I would probably still be a miserable lawyer. Likewise, thanks to Ben, Josh, Mike, Clayton, and Chris for getting me out of the law and into writing about politics. Thanks to Kenny for letting me fill in once on the radio, which really gave me the opportunity to find out what I wanted to do in life. Thanks to my friends and compatriots at RedState and The Resurgent for being willing to defend me, encourage me, and pick up the slack for me while I have been writing this book.

To Michelle, Lucy, John, and Sam for opening the doors to CNN and letting me in. To David, Donna, James, Mary, and Paul for taking me under their care—showing me that we can disagree on politics and still be friends. To Anderson and Wolf for putting up with me for so long and being willing to engage a view not often heard on news shows.

To Sean Hannity, Bill Shine, and the late Roger Ailes for welcoming me over to Fox, thank you.

Rush Limbaugh, James Golden, and Kraig Kitchin deserve a world of thanks. They let me sit behind the golden EIB microphone. I really do not know that Rush appreciates how much I value him as a friend and mentor. Still one of the greatest pieces of advice I ever got, I got from him—to make sure I had someone around to tell me when I had screwed up, because at some point, if things went in the right direction, everyone would just want to suck up. That is so true. While I am thanking people in radio, both Mark Levin and Glenn Beck have been so supportive this past year and willing to send notes of encouragement. Even when we disagree on an issue, we are friendly in disagreement.

Thank you, Charlie, my producer, for being a jerk when I need it and always a friend, and thank you, Philip and Candice, for managing my schedule and directing my attention so that I could write. Thanks too to Andrew, who makes me sound way better on the radio than I should. I may have a face for radio, but I have a voice for print. Thank you, Bill, who cowrote my last book with me and encouraged me to put my keys on the keyboard solo for this go-round.

Thank you, Pete and Donna, for standing by me through the storms that have engulfed me and my family. You are both great bosses and even better friends. It is a pleasure to go to work and view that work as a hobby, but the downside is it makes the balance between family and work harder. I could not ask to work with better people. Everyone at Cox has been so supportive through this time. It is nice to work for a company that treats you like family.

Russell Moore and his team at the ERLC have been great prayer warriors of mine in the last year and have encouraged me to write about my faith and life during this trying time. They really led me to write the essay that caught David Brooks's attention. David, likewise, whom I have only met once, in passing, deserves thanks. This book would not have happened but for his kind mention of it in his column.

I cannot name all my friends and listeners who have prayed for my family during this time, but they are owed a great deal of thanks. A special thank-you to my small band of brothers— they know who they are—who serve as an accountability group and support group.

Lastly, Paul Whitlatch, my editor, has been wonderful to work with. He has been supportive and given great direction along the way. It was a refreshing experience and leaves me for once finishing a book thinking I could do another one, instead of wanting to never have anything to do again with writing. Keith and Matt, thanks for connecting us, rooting for me, and thinking this was a good idea. It has been a cathartic experience to write this.

# LIST OF RECIPES

# MEATS

# THANKSGIVING

# DESSERTS

Books are produced in the United States using U.S.-based materials

Books are printed using a revolutionary new process called THINKtech™ that lowers energy usage by 70% and increases overall quality

Books are durable and flexible because of smythe-sewing

Paper is sourced using environmentally responsible foresting methods and the paper is acid-free

**Center Point Large Print**
600 Brooks Road / PO Box 1
Thorndike, ME 04986-0001 USA

**(207) 568-3717**

**US & Canada:**
**1 800 929-9108**
**www.centerpointlargeprint.com**